D1263894

HELL IN THE STREETS
OF HUSAYBAH

HELL IN THE STREETS OF HUSAYBAH

The April 2004 Fights of 3rd Battalion,
7th Marines in Husaybah, Iraq

By Lieutenant Colonel David E. Kelly,
USMC, Retired

CASEMATE

Philadelphia & Oxford

Published in the United States of America and Great Britain in 2022 by
CASEMATE PUBLISHERS
1950 Lawrence Road, Havertown, PA 19083, USA
and
The Old Music Hall, 106–108 Cowley Road, Oxford OX4 1JE, UK

Hardback Edition: ISBN 978-1-63624-150-0
Digital Edition: ISBN 978-1-63624-151-7

A CIP record for this book is available from the British Library

Printed and bound in the United States of America by Integrated Books International

Typeset in India by Lapiz Digital Services, Chennai.

For a complete list of Casemate titles, please contact:

CASEMATE PUBLISHERS (US)
Telephone (610) 853-9131
Fax (610) 853-9146
Email: casemate@casematepublishers.com
www.casematepublishers.com

CASEMATE PUBLISHERS (UK)
Telephone (01865) 241249
Email: casemate-uk@casematepublishers.co.uk
www.casematepublishers.co.uk

Contents

Dedication

This book is dedicated to two groups:

The officers and men of the Third Battalion, Seventh Marine
Regiment (3/7) who welcomed me on my arrival at their remote
base camp near the Syrian border crossing. Lieutenant Colonel
Matthew Lopez and his battalion staff insured that I met with many
key individuals involved in the frenetic and challenging operations
that occurred in the middle of April 2004 at Husaybah, Iraq.

I was honored to record their accounts of danger,
heroism, and careful decision-making.

Also, my family who supported me in my desire to deploy to
Iraq as a field historian after being retired from the Marine Corps
Reserve for almost 4 years. My wife Terrie Kelly, and daughters
Donna Kelly Romero and Rosie Kelly Sullivan knew that this
was a chance for me to contribute to the Marine Corps efforts to
capture first hand accounts by Marines during operations in Iraq.

DAVID E. KELLY, Lieutenant Colonel, USMC, Retired

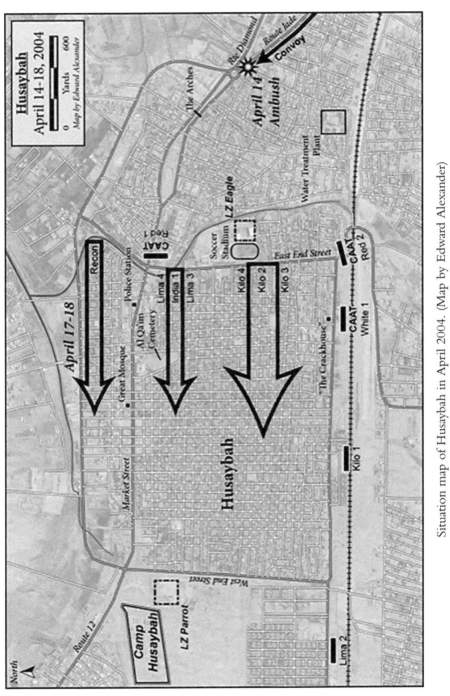

Situation map of Husaybah in April 2004. (Map by Edward Alexander)

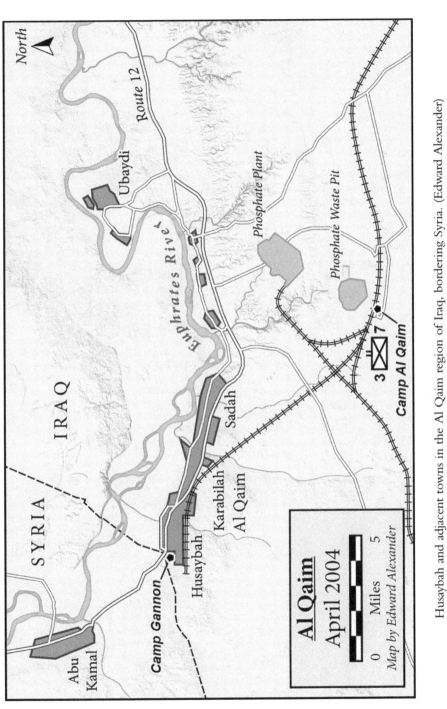

Husaybah and adjacent towns in the Al Qaim region of Iraq, bordering Syria. (Edward Alexander)

Preface

The Marine Corps Oral History Program dates back to 1965 when the Corps became heavily involved in Vietnam. Its mission is to document Marine Corps history as it happens, by interviewing Marines involved in current operations. Field historians capture the experiences and perspectives of Marines of all ranks, along with photographs, maps and documents, to preserve history before it is lost. As a result, the program has produced a large collection of field interviews that detail the role of Marines in operations and developments from 1965 to the present.

Along with Major John Piedmont, I was one of two Marine Corps field historians sent to Iraq in the spring of 2004. We were both Reserve officers from the Marine Corps History and Museums Division located in Washington, DC. Our Letter of Instruction, the official document that outlined our mission, was clear: To travel throughout the Marine Area of Responsibility (AOR) in Iraq, and conduct field history interviews with Marines and sailors. We had no quotas to meet. We did not attach to any individual unit. This allowed us the freedom to meet with Marines at all ranks and staff levels, to try and flesh out official reports with the words of these Marines. Future researchers and historians may find this information valuable as they reconstruct the events in Iraq during 2004.

What made our work possible was the cooperation that we met at every level of command in IMEF (1st Marine Expeditionary Force). The command gave us access to meet with Marines in every part of Iraq. Use of the military internet and land line phone systems allowed us to inform units that we were in-bound, and gave them time to select key individuals for us to interview. As the senior member of the field history team, I created a matrix of all of the major command elements under IMEF, and attempted to visit each command at least once during our five-month deployment.

Our deployment began in May 2004 with a commercial flight into Kuwait at Camp Wolverine, and there we made arrangements to fly into Iraq by military transport. Once in Iraq, we began our work, using Camp Fallujah as our base of operations.

Major Piedmont and I were able to meet with Marines at Husaybah and Camp Al Qaim. I began with the battalion commander of 3/7, Lieutenant Colonel Matthew Allen Lopez, and went down to Marine fire team leaders and members of supporting units. Each Marine and sailor creates a picture of the events as they happened from his perspective. The audio recordings are history "in the raw," recorded within weeks of the events. I hope that this approach will allow the reader to gain an appreciation for the dedication and accomplishments of these Marines and sailors, as well as the effort and teamwork required in these actions far from home. I also explain how we field historians went to the front to gather these accounts.

I later reviewed the oral history interviews that I conducted, and now present them in the order that they were done. They are written in a combination of narrative and direct quotes to make them more accessible to non-military readers. After combining my official journal, interview notes and interview transcriptions, I have attempted to create a sense of the actions and thoughts of these Marines who fought in Husaybah and adjacent areas in April 2004.

Introduction

"Lima 5 is now Lima 6."

CAPTAIN DOMINIQUE NEAL, CAMP HUSAYBAH, APRIL 17, 2004

This radio message on April 17, 2004 encapsulated much of what was underway in a small town on the Iraq–Syria border. These words signaled that the Lima Company commanding officer had been killed in combat operations, and that the executive officer now assumed command. Lima Company, 3rd Battalion 7th Marine Regiment, was the focal point of events in the town of Husaybah that month.

Much has been written about events in Iraq during and after the rapid invasion phase of the conflict in the spring of 2003. On the Marine Corps side, the combat units left within months of the successful overthrow of the regime of Saddam Hussein. In early 2004 the Marine Corps sent the 1st Marine Expeditionary Force (1MEF) back to Iraq with the goal of conducting Security and Stability Operations (SASO), mainly in the Al Anbar province of Iraq.

In March 2004, a smoldering insurgency erupted throughout Iraq, starting with the slaying and defiling of the bodies of American contractors in the city of Fallujah. By April, a full-scale insurgency broke out in many parts of that nation. Planned Security and Stability Operations were put on hold as American forces began to conduct full-scale military operations. The focus for the American news media was the city of Fallujah. This city's location, close to the Iraqi capital of Baghdad, made it easy for media members to go there and send reports back to the U.S. Also, as Fallujah is a relatively big city, and had a large American force stationed just outside its boundaries, military events there loomed large.

Meanwhile, far west of Fallujah on the border with Syria, a similar uprising took place in the city of Husaybah. A much smaller urban area than Fallujah, it nonetheless was also the scene of intense fighting in mid-April 2004. One Marine battalion, 3/7, along with attachments, fought to destroy an uprising there.

They fought fiercely. Battalion Commander Matthew Lopez's Humvee was targeted by hidden rockets as he entered the city. Lima Company Commander Captain Richard Gannon was killed by enemy fire while leading his men into an enemy-held building. Corporal Jason Dunham was awarded the Congressional Medal of Honor when he sacrificed his life to save those of his fellow Marines from an enemy grenade. The Marines of 3/7 conducted a two-day clearance of a whole city, going room to room, building to building, to search out enemy fighters.

Perhaps because this was a much smaller city, or because of its distance from media outlets, the battle of Husaybah received very little outside notice. But the Marines of 3/7 fought intensely in the first battle of Husaybah. It is a story that should be told. This book is a small part of this effort.

CHAPTER I

Lieutenant Colonel Lopez, Commanding Officer, 3/7

Monday May 31, 2004: Camp Al Assad

In the spring of 2004, travel around the Al Anbar region of Iraq required planning and coordination. Almost all of our travel to other distant Marine camps was done on Marine helicopters. In the eastern portion of Al Anbar, these trips took place at night to provide greater security for the aircraft.

After a night ride on a Marine CH46 helo from Camp Fallujah to Camp Al Assad, Major Piedmont and I began the day at the RCT7 Command Post, with a tour of their Combat Operations Center (COC). Major Bill Zeman showed us through the building. Using a huge wall map, he gave us an overview of RCT7's operations in western Al Anbar Province: their Area of Operations (AO) was about the size of Wyoming. He briefed us on the April 2004 battle in Husaybah. I would soon meet many of the Marines who participated in this action.

The COC itself was nicely laid out by Master Sergeant Garcia, who explained how he built up several platforms for desks so that all of the battalion staff and watch officers had a good view of briefing maps and materials. We then briefly met the S3 operations officer, Lieutenant Colonel Nicholas Vuckovitch, the executive officer (XO), Lieutenant Colonel Gamboa, and finally the regimental commander of 7th Marines, Colonel Craig Tucker. We tried to schedule interviews with them today, but the flight to Al Qaim was supposed to leave in early afternoon, so we deferred on interviews until a return trip.

All afternoon it was on again, off again, with the Al Qaim flight. From Al Assad to western parts of Al Anbar, the Marine Corps used its large CH 53 Echo helicopters for combat service support. This area was largely open desert, which allowed for daytime flights. Our destination, Al Qaim, was about 114 miles away.

Fortunately, the battalion commander of 3/7, Lieutenant Colonel Matt Lopez, was also waiting for the same helos, and we seized the opportunity to interview him. The interview gave us both an introduction to 3/7's operations, and some background for questions when we arrived at Al Qaim.

* * *

Lieutenant Colonel Matthew Allen Lopez Commanding Officer, 3rd Battalion, 7th Marine Regiment (3/7)

While we waited for our flight to Al Qaim, Lieutenant Colonel Lopez invited us to ride with him as he went to Al Assad's military exchange. On our return to the flight line to wait for the helos, I interviewed in the truck he was using while Major Piedmont interviewed the battalion sergeant major. Good use of our downtime. Plus, the truck was air-conditioned and it was a quiet place for the interview. This began our look at events in Husaybah that took place in the first half of 2004.

After being selected for command, Lieutenant Colonel Lopez took over 3/7 in June 2003. During Operation Iraqi Freedom I (OIF I) he wound up as the military governor of Karbala, Iraq, with a task force of about 1,600 Marines, soldiers and sailors. "We left Karbala, Iraq, on September 15th of 2003, and returned here. Departed the United States on 13th February [2004] to come back to OIF II-1. The good thing about coming back right away is 70 percent of my battalion are the same Marines that served with us in Karbala, Iraq. My entire battalion staff other than my S1 [Administration and Personnel] and S6 [Command and Information Systems] are the same Marine officers and mostly Staff NCOs that we had in OIF I."

The battle for Husaybah has been the biggest event for his battalion this year. It began on April 14, with an enemy-led ambush. About

25 enemy fighters fired a couple of dozen RPGs and sustained small arms fire for a 30-minute firefight. "That occurred on the command group and the Civil Affairs group that was moving in between police stations, trying to set up training for the local Iraqi police force. At the same time that was occurring, there were smaller attacks throughout the town of Husaybah. And it ended up being a three-to-four-hour offensive on our part to destroy the enemy and some of the ambushes that we were in. The Marines did extremely well on the 14th."

Their biggest actions took place on April 17 and 18 in Husaybah. Lopez explained that Al Qaim is the name of the area that includes several towns, with a total population of about 230,000. The largest city, Husaybah, has about 30,000 inhabitants. Husaybah sits on Route 12, and is one of the main points of entry into Iraq from Syria. "One of our critical tasks is to guard that Iraqi outpost on the border with Syria.

"The enemy kicked it off at 0800 precisely, where they conducted a mortar attack, where about 25 to 30 mortar rounds impacted on the Battalion Task Force main effort, which is Lima Company. Lima Company has a company-size task force that mans that border checkpoint between Syria and Iraq."

Lima had about 230 Marines in this task force. Lopez said that mortar attacks on that compound were not uncommon when they arrived in Iraq. There would be about 25 to 30 rounds hit every day, but that had slowed down to three to four rounds, two or three days a week.

"Fortunately, we had sniper positions in the city, and we were able to detect where the mortar rounds were comin' from, and Marines from Force Recon that are in direct support of my task force, were chopped down to Lima, 3/7, in the town of Husaybah, and they were able to engage and kill five individuals that were conducting a mortar attack on Lima Company."

During the mortar attack, Lima Company had sent out a QRF (Quick Reaction Force) into the northeast section of Husaybah and it became engaged in a large-size ambush with about 15 individuals who fired RPGs (rocket-propelled grenades) and small arms. The up-armored Humvees received many small arms hits, but the armor prevented serious wounds to Lima's Marines. While this was happening, the sniper team that had just eliminated the enemy mortar position came under intense ground fire from two different sides of the building where they had established their OP (observation post).

"We got word of the combined attack back at the CP [command post]. I was actually at a police graduation, an Iraqi police graduation; we were graduating our first class of 47 new Iraqi police officers. I had moved out to visit one of the police stations, and by 10:30 in the morning I was positioned at the northeast corner of Husaybah. We call it Market Street and East End."

A Lima Company platoon that was patrolling joined in the fight at the OP. Some of the fighting involved tossing grenades inside of the building occupied by the OP. Some enemy had moved into the lower floor of a building occupied by Marines on upper floors. This fight lasted from about 0830 until 1030.

"We were later to find out that that enemy force was there as an ambush force for any reaction force on an attack that came later in the morning on the actual Firm Base itself [Lima Company's position]."

CAAT (Combined Anti-Armor Team) sections were sent out to support the platoon at the OP.

"Corporal Gibson, at the time, was hit by small arms fire from an AK 47, and as he and three of his team members were being moved to safety inside a house, Captain Gannon [Lima Company's commanding officer] followed them inside that house, and all five of these Marines ended up getting killed within that house there."

This house was adjacent to the house used as the Marine OP, and the Marines had entered it to help the Marines in the OP. Along with Captain Gannon, Lance Corporal Smith, Lance Corporal Looven, Lance Corporal Valdez, and Corporal Gibson died inside the house.

"We believe that the first three were killed with AK fire as they came in, and Captain Gannon followed them in, and he was also hit with RPK [light machine gun]. That was an enemy strongpoint." Lieutenant Colonel Lopez learned of Captain Gannon's death about the time that he arrived that morning in Husaybah.

Lieutenant Colonel Lopez then radioed back to the battalion CP and called for the battalion QRF to move to Husaybah. "I wasn't really sure yet about the extent and the size of the enemy attack, but we knew that there was a very well-coordinated attack on the northeast corner of town, at the same time we had reports that enemy forces—which is the first time that they donned actual uniforms—many of the enemy, for the first time ever that day, were wearing a black pajamas uniform and a traditional red and white khaffiyah on their heads."

Lopez received reports from the Lima Company executive officer that about 200 enemy fighters were three blocks east of the company's Firm Base. "Then we realized, for the first time, the scale of this, that somebody was actually attacking to take over the city itself." Additionally, Intel reports came in about 10:30 that morning that said that imminent insurgent targets included a police station, and the local government headquarters, as well as an attack to overrun Lima Company's Firm Base on the Syrian border. "There was some intense fighting on the east side of the city all morning as we prepared ourselves to do an assault through the city."

By 1200 Lieutenant Colonel Lopez called in Kilo Company from Al Qaim to move to Husaybah. By 1300, he moved Kilo Company's two platoons to the southern portion of the east section of Husaybah. Lima Company formed the middle sector, and he made the Force Recon unit (along with two ODA—Special Forces—teams) into a third maneuver element. Weapons Company established a casualty collection point and rear security along East End (a soccer stadium).

"With Weapons Company covering our rear, we conducted an assault across the city. We fought across the city from 1700 until approximately 2100. By that time, we reached what we called the 'West End,' a major road that runs right in front of the Lima Company Firm Base. Early on in the fighting there were many Iraqis who owned AK 47s, could pick up AK 47s and fire them at Marines as we moved across the city. The major pocket of resistance was right there, three to four blocks to the east of what we call 'West End'. And there were actually, what I would consider Anti-Coalition Forces, an organized military-type force that created that strong point. It took about an hour to go the last three blocks."

Lieutenant Colonel Lopez had a platoon at Lima Company's Firm Base, with the company XO (executive officer) commanding it, maneuver towards a building that was reported to be an enemy command point. When they confirmed that the target building was indeed being used as a command point, they hit it with 81mm mortar fire. It gave Lopez great confidence in the Intel reports he had received. "It really gave us a good picture of what we were about ready to face in town." He also said that his interpreter at the time was a local Iraqi who was able to get on his Iridium phone and cell phone and call around the city and find out what was going on. "He provided absolute perfect intelligence to me, where enemy forces were massing, and what their array was on the battlefield.

"Lieutenant Carroll and his two platoons, his company minus, they ran into the stiffest resistance, and we were able to maneuver Force Recon, who had a tough fight on the north side of Market Street. But they were able to push up and actually turn the corner. So, where the stiffest resistance was, we had Lieutenant Carroll attacking from east to west, at the same time Force Recon was able to turn the corner and provide supporting fires as Lieutenant Carroll hit that main line of resistance."

Lieutenant Colonel Lopez also reinforced Lieutenant Carroll's force with an entire MP platoon that had eight hardened vehicles with .50 caliber machine guns on them. During the fight for the city, they had continuous rotary wing close air support that followed smoke markers on the ground to find designated targets.

"Cobras [Bell AH-1W attack helicopters] did a phenomenal job on that day with close-in fire support." He added that in many cases this "close-in" support was within 50 feet of friendly units operating in the city. They also had fixed-wing CAS (close air support), but could not use them because of the presence of a city full of innocent civilians and non-combatants as well as the fact that the Marines were fighting so close to enemy positions. Lopez felt that this decision paid dividends as the inhabitants saw that the Marines would only use the force necessary to destroy enemy fighters, and not destroy their city. He said that this was an IO (Information Operations) victory as well.

By about 1900 that night, the battalion consolidated on the western part of Husaybah. The battalion and its attachments established a cordon around the city, and no one could enter or leave. The enemy tried a small counterattack at about 0100 in the morning on the southeast part of the city, but a blocking position with CAAT Red under Lieutenant Inglehart and Staff Sergeant Kelly called in Cobras and destroyed this attack almost before it began. Throughout the rest of this fighting, 3/7 had 17 WIA, and no additional KIAs.

At about 0330, Lieutenant Colonel Lopez's command group was leaving the LZ area (landing zone for helos) and received some fire from an anti-aircraft gun from the direction of Syria, just west of Husaybah.

"The next morning, we swept with Lima Company, now reassembled, and with the former XO, Lieutenant Dominique Neal. [I] placed him in charge of the company sometime around 0330; by 0900, they were again sweeping from north to south across the city, with a cordon of Weapons Company, Force Recon and MP Platoon still in place, and with Kilo Company on their right flank [to the west]." He said that there was no strong resistance that day, and some enemy forces tried to escape out of the city to the east, but the blocking forces prevented this.

During the fighting on April 17, Lieutenant Colonel Lopez estimated that his Marines ran into a total of about 25 IEDs (improvised explosive devices) and found another 17 or so the next day. Marines received sporadic fire on the 18th. He estimated that there were at least 150 enemy fighters, and possibly as many as 300. "Pretty confident that we killed at least 120." He also noted that about 20 innocent civilians were caught up in the fighting and killed.

On the morning of April 19, Lopez allowed ambulances into the city to pick up dead bodies and to assist the wounded to get into hospitals. Many locals were shaken up by the fighting, but also upset that the insurgent fighters had instigated this fight with the Marines. Later reports let him know that there were about 25 foreign fighters leading the fight, as well as about 100 Iraqis from outside the Husaybah area.

Lieutenant Colonel Lopez was especially proud of the actions of his officers and Marines that day, and many award commendations have been submitted for heroic actions.

At 0900 on April 19, Lopez lifted the curfew and cordon of the city of Husaybah, and allowed people to go about their business as normal. "Our support from the local people, kind, unbelieving to me was better after the attack than it had ever been to that point. For 30 days after the attack there was not a single direct-fire engagement, or IED engagement with coalition forces. I'm sure any enemy or any anti-coalition forces fled the area after the defeat they were given. Since then, it's returned back to where, you know, on a bad day we'll experience up to 12 IEDs in one day, but the average is probably about four or five IEDs a day. Last evening, that would be the 30th, was the first time we saw a direct fire engagement with an RPG since the day of the 17th." RPG fire had been a daily occurrence before the 17th.

Lieutenant Colonel Lopez said that because of the relative quiet during those 30 days, his battalion was able to accomplish many of the things that they had originally set out to do, including training up ICDC (Iraqi Civil Defense Corps) forces and the local police, and beginning civil affairs projects in earnest. Previously it had been hard to get the local Iraqis to cooperate with the Marines on projects due to the threat from the insurgents. He said that before the 17th, Al Qaim had been one of the most hostile areas, and since then has been one of the most peaceful.

"We look forward to the 1st of July Turnover [of sovereignty to the Iraqi Provisional Government]." But he knew that there were many questions to be answered as to what this would mean for the people of Iraq. He said that he didn't expect as much offensive combat as he has encountered, but has been able to quell that for the time being, and has gotten to accomplish the mission of establishing the local government and local security forces. His Marines have done joint patrols with the ICDC and the Iraqi police.

"The Iraqi border police are doing a superb job in our area, ICDC is probably one of the strongest in Iraq right now, but we're still a little bit further behind on Iraq police because it's hard to break 35 years of the fact that the police were part of the problem."

Asked whether the ICDC stayed on their posts during the fighting in the city, he replied: "The Iraqi police were an absolute non-factor. The Iraqi Civil Defense Corps, they stayed in their compound, and then, I actually tasked them to provide a blocking position between Lima Company's position in Husaybah at the border checkpoint and north to the river. When it turned into full-out combat, it was safer for them not to be out on the street because of their limited training, limited experience, and the fact that it wasn't a full-out enemy uniform that you could actually distinguish between the two. I actually told the ICDC commander to keep his people off the street, and we put them in a blocking position … on our northern flank." They manned it, and after the 18th they helped to collect the dead enemy in the city. Since then, the ICDC, who had been resistant to doing joint patrols, have been doing two daytime and two nighttime patrols with the Marines every day. The ICDC has also begun to mentor the local Iraqi police in doing patrolling.

I then asked Lieutenant Colonel Lopez about preparing for this return to Iraq. It began in September of 2003, with squad-level training. In the summer of 2003, he had lost some 300 NCOs (to transfers, EAS (End of Active Service), etc.), so the small-unit training was very much needed. Many of the squad leaders were veterans of Karbala, and had real-world experience. From December on, the training began at a high level. Then the battalion went on a two-week regimental training exercise. The 14-day training package was called "Lane Training," and included individual skills, fire team skills, and squad skills. Urban patrolling, MOUT (Military Operations in Urban Terrain), Mounted Patrolling Urban Environment, and offensive combat were all taught and rehearsed.

"We really focused on what we called the Five Golden Rules: We set out early in my command here, that no patrol would go out without a combat mentality." The rules included writing proper Five-Paragraph

Orders, pre-combat inpections, rehearsals, confirmation briefs, and proper debriefs.

In January the battalion went through Division-run training at March Air Force Base, then returned to its base and did extensive live-fire training. Lieutenant Colonel Lopez emphasized the basics of Marine infantry operations: SMEAC, Warning Order, Five-Paragraph Orders, proper pre-combat checks and inspections, proper rehearsals, proper confirmation brief, and proper de-brief. He sent his Marines on leave from December 21 until January 5, 2004.

"I tell all my Marines that we'll get home when we get home." He had expected the deployment to be more dangerous this time, with a lot more resistance to the presence of the Marines. But he felt that his battalion—located about a three-and-a-half-hour drive from the regimental CP—has really been able to turn the opinion of the local Iraqis towards the Marines.

Lieutenant Colonel Lopez said, "I don't think anybody can honestly say that combat and what we went through is what they expected." It is an unpredictable area, here on the Syrian border, and very volatile.

Lopez offered some final thoughts: "What I'll take away from this is how brilliant the individual Marine performs. Throughout our history, time and time again, you know, it's the individual Marine and his ability to meet the challenge, to meet the danger, and just absolutely perform beyond your wildest expectations. When the time came for them to perform, they performed, and they performed magnificently. And they continue to do so on a daily basis. Their motivation and their level of dedication, you just can't even comprehend that until you see them go into all-out combat like that, and then 48 hours later turn around and start aiding the people that just hours prior to that might have been shooting at them. Their ability to go from, it's a cliché, 'No better friend, no worse enemy,' but to see them transition from that no worse enemy, back to the no better friend was really pretty amazing.

"I guess when you lose men, especially a company commander, well any Marine, when you lose men in combat, you always question what the long-term benefit of them paying the ultimate sacrifice will be. That chapter's yet to be written."

★ ★ ★

Interview concluded, Lieutenant Colonel Lopez, Major Piedmont and I rode back up to the flight line and soon boarded a CH53 Echo to take us to Al Qaim in daylight.

The chopper had a load of equipment in the center of the compartment, so we climbed around the gear and sat on the side seats. The ride was uneventful as we flew over mile after mile of bright yellow-brown desert, with very little sign of life other than some occasional scrub brush. Even so, the flight crew kept a watch out for any potential ground fire at us.

At 3/7's COC, Captain Rory Quinn from the S3 shop met us, got us situated with our gear (I was given the VIP visitor's room on the second floor), and then gave us an overview of the battalion's AO on a wall map, and operations the battalion has been doing since its arrival in early March 2004. After chow, Major Piedmont interviewed the S3 as I listened. By the time the day ended, we both had a fair grasp of 3/7's operations. It was time to grab some sleep so we'd be fresh for a day full of interviews.

CHAPTER 2

Marines of 3/7

Tuesday June 1, 2004: Camp Al Qaim

The buildings used by 3/7 at Camp Al Qaim were an Iraqi train station and rail yard that had been taken over by the battalion. The battalion S3 had prepared a detailed itinerary of who would see us for interviews. This schedule started at 1000 each day, and went until well after dark.

I let the Marines know that the interviews would be one-on-one, and gave them estimated times to be ready to meet me. They could "stand by" in the area while they waited. Given their hectic schedules, they probably welcomed the chance to grab some rest while waiting.

Commander Edward William Hessel, MD, USN
Officer in Charge of STP 4, Camp Al Qaim

I first walked over to STP 4 (Shock Trauma Platoon), where I got a tour of the facility and then did an interview with the OIC (officer in charge), Commander Hessel. The unit was set up in a series of large tents, with treatment areas, operating and recovery areas, all air-conditioned.

Commander Hessel is an emergency room physician, a graduate of the University of Oregon. He did his residency with the Navy, and served with Marine Wing units before his first deployment to Iraq. In OIF I, he served in Iraq at Al Qaim and Jalaba. In November 2004 he learned that medical personnel from the Naval Medical Center, San Diego, would be deploying to Iraq.

I asked him to explain how the Shock Trauma Platoon is organized. He said that currently there are 20 personnel in the platoon, including a critical care nurse, Lieutenant Ted Herring, USN, and a physician's assistant, Lieutenant Pat Hare, USN. There is also an independent duty Corpsman, eight general purpose Corpsmen, and seven Marines who are the drivers, mechanics, and security. The STP is capable of mobile operations, but they have been stationary since setting up here at Al Qaim.

Commander Hessel initially met his team on February 5, and they deployed on February 14, 2004. They spent a short time at Camp Victory, but still did not have all of their equipment until they got to Al Assad.

"The way the STP was set up, we have initial, three resuscitation areas, run by myself, the other physician and the physician's assistant. And with that we have two Corpsmen at each station, and then we also have Evac tents, and a Minimal tent that is run next to the Resuscitation tent. We have assigned Corpsmen for their specific duties there. We also have our Marines that assist us, not only as stretcher carriers, but a couple of the Marines are interested in medical care. We've done some cross-training with them on some splinting, IV techniques, and they have also been involved in patient care with some of the Marines."

His team arrived at Al Qaim on the evening of March 11, and had the STP up and running by March 12. "The next day we started to receive our first casualties. And, it was fairly steady. We were getting casualties just about every other day for the time period through March. And then we had a peak time in April, and I think to this point we've treated over 50 casualties to this point in STP."

Commander Hessel said that the heaviest day so far was when STP treated 12 casualties at once. A determination is made there whether to send a casualty to the FRSS (Forward Resuscitative Surgery System) at Al Qaim, or on to the CASH (Combat Support Hospital) in Baghdad. He said that they have been seeing a lot of penetrating head and neck injuries here, which are best treated at a Level 3 facility such as the CASH in Baghdad.

When I first met him at the STP area, he took me on a tour of the facility. I asked for a verbal tour of the STP on the recording. He explained that when he first got here, wounded Marines were brought by helo to an LZ, and then transferred by Humvee to the STP. Within a month, they made a helo pad only about 200 feet away from the FRSS, so now the Marines and Corpsmen carried the wounded directly to the Resuscitation tent. In this tent, the teams determined whether to send the wounded on to the FRSS, if they could be stabilized or moved to the Evac tent, or if they needed follow-on and a flight to the CASH. The US Army's 507th, the Air Ambulance Group, provides quick response time in moving wounded to the STP and on to the CASH if needed. "The response of the 507th in getting the wounded from Husaybah has been spectacular. Sometimes we get these patients within 20 to 25 minutes of their initial injury."

This Army detachment is here to provide a CASEVAC (casualty evacuation) capability for the Marines. They have Blackhawk helicopters with oxygen and medical equipment on board, and their two crew chiefs are trained almost to the level of paramedics. The Army crew can care for patients on board. "If we have to utilize Marine assets to lift them [the wounded] from here, which we have done on several occasions, that usually involved putting one of our critical care nurses on board, or one of our Corpsmen on board, to go onto Al Assad, and then we have lost them for a period of time." Hessel said that by having the 507th, "We've probably done a lot of stuff we couldn't have done without them here."

I asked about the number of his personnel who have been to the Theater before. His critical care nurse was at Kuwait, and about four of his Marines were in Iraq with other STPs, as was one HM1 (Corpsman). In 2003, Commander Hessel was in Al Jabr with Marine aviation. They used C130s to do long-range medevac, moving 107 patients through there. But he said, "We have treated more Marines than we did in OIF I." He has treated 50 Marine casualties to date.

He described the April 2004 events as a crescendo that then slowed down. The busiest day had 12 wounded Marines. Three surgeries were done in one day, and more serious wounds were sent on to Al Assad or the CASH in Baghdad. In at least one case, Corpsmen were doing significant medical emergency resuscitation, as the doctors were busy with other wounded Marines. "That was fast and furious, I think it only took four or five hours to treat all those wounds or move them on."

Since late April things have been relatively slow. Some of the routine wounds have gone through the Battalion Aid Station (BAS). There was a three-week period starting in late April with almost no treatment needed at the STP.

The helo LZ is now near the STP, but the tents are in a courtyard-like area. The tents are buttoned up when helos land, as they kick up a lot of dust and pebbles.

Commander Hessel added, "I couldn't be more proud of what these guys are doing. They're asked to do some pretty—they assume a lot of responsibility here, and they have performed every single time. And they come together as a team when we work. And that's the thing I think I've been most proud about—that they are doing a really good job."

He finished by saying that the Marines here know that the STP brings good medical care when needed. "If we can get these casualties within 20 minutes, we can accomplish a lot." Also, the Corpsmen and Marines in the field have been able to provide excellent first aid treatment for chest wounds, broken bones, etc. "It's a good group to work with and to work for."

Lance Corporal Jason Alan Sanders
Platoon Radio Operator and Mortar Section Leader, 4th Platoon, Kilo Company, 3/7

This young Marine's life was saved, along with other Marines, by Corporal Jason Dunham, who threw himself on top of a grenade tossed by an insurgent. Dunham died as a result of his heroic action. (President George W. Bush presented Corporal Dunham's parents with Dunham's Medal of Honor on January 11 2007, at the White House.)

Lance Corporal Sanders began recruit training in March 2002 and deployed to OIF I in January 2003, with Kilo Company, 3/7. He said that prior to returning to Iraq, the training revolved around SASO, IED awareness and training, with crew-served weapons training minimized. In March 2004, Kilo Company arrived in Kuwait and spent two weeks there. They moved to Al Assad, and then to what the Army called FOB (Forward Operating Base) Tiger, now known to the Marines as Camp Al Qaim. To do the turnover with the Army units here, he said, "One platoon went to Husaybah on the border, and they had a border checkpoint up there. Lima [Company] went up there to learn how to work the border. They did mechanized patrols up there and we were the first to do a foot patrol in that AO in a long time." After a couple of weeks, the Army departed.

Once the Marines were here on their own: "We [Kilo Company] were doin' patrols in Husaybah for one month, doin' a rotation with Lima. Two platoons up there from Kilo Company, 1st and 4th Platoon." They did presence patrols, civil affairs patrols, in general showing a Marine presence on foot in the town. There were two patrols a day, four hours each. There was no participation by any Iraqi units in these patrols. Lance Corporal Sanders' platoon then came back to Al Qaim.

Patrols with the Iraqi Police (IP) began after about this first month. Things were pretty smooth until about April 14, when Corporal Jason Dunham went out with his squad along with the CO of Kilo Company to do a leader's recon of a water treatment facility of a Forward Operating Base in Karabilah.

"We heard mortar fire and some small arms fire back to the west towards Husaybah, so we went ahead, got mounted up, and started pushing towards Husaybah. We dismounted right at the arches before Husaybah, started workin' our way into the HK triangle heading south, and then had a VCP [Vehicle Checkpoint] set up on East End, which is in Husaybah, and pushed all the traffic that was tryin' to avoid that up the HK where we were working our patrol towards."

Then Dunham's squad decided to start searching cars that were avoiding the VCP. Lance Corporal Sanders saw Corporal Dunham take an individual to the ground, and they were wrestling around.

"I was two men behind him, and another guy on the left side. It was Lance Corporal Hampton and then Lance Corporal Miller; both ran up to assist him [Dunham]. The guy ... musta had a grenade. He did have a grenade! I heard something about the hands, muffled something about the hands, 'Watch the hands,' or somethin' along like that. And then ... the grenade blew up. Lance Corporal Hampton and Miller were, everybody was knocked unconscious, and Lance Corporal Hampton and Miller got up and walked back behind me to a CCP [casualty collection point] that was established. I hollered, 'Staff Sergeant, Dunham's left!' I hollered at him to cover me while I went down to get Corporal Dunham. He was still out. He was still on the deck. Went down to get him. The Iraqi that had the grenade was knocked out, but he got up and started running. [I] shot him and killed him."

Corporal Dunham was then brought back to the CCP. Sanders started taking some small arms fire while Staff Sergeant Ferguson started to suppress this with his own weapon. They got Dunham to the CASEVAC area, and started to administer first aid to him. Marines came and took Dunham to the helicopters for medevac.

I then asked Lance Corporal Sanders to describe in more detail Corporal Dunham's actions that day. He replied, "He saw the guy [Iraqi], he knew the guy had somethin', and he was right up on him. From what I saw, the only course of action he could have taken, since he was so close to him, without getting anybody else hurt, was for him to jump on the guy, either try to get the grenade away, or just shield it with his body. Or, shield it with his helmet, and by the looks of his helmet afterwards, I'm gonna go with that theory. He did try to cover [I interjected, "He took it off?"], try to cover it with his helmet, yes sir."

Sanders said that the other two Marines were right up there with him, and Dunham's actions definitely saved their lives. "It was all one big pile, and two definitely were saved." Sanders added that the Iraqi insurgent had gotten out of the car, and clearly wanted to kill several Marines if he could.

"When I went up to drag Corporal Dunham back, I glanced over [at the insurgent's car], and this is before the vehicle is even searched, a grenade was laying on the floor, and then afterwards there were RPG with a couple warheads, and some small arms."

Dunham was still alive at this time. "I was still talking to him. He didn't answer me, I didn't know the extent of the injuries until afterwards, but I was talking to him the whole time, when I got him back up the hill, he was breathing. The doc that was there said he was breathing, and after I got him out of the kill zone, I was just worried about getting the bird [helo] to him, sir."

Corporal Dunham was then moved to Al Qaim, then to Al Assad, then Baghdad. He died about six to eight days later at a hospital in Germany, with his family near him.

We both paused briefly before I continued my questions.

Three days later, April 17, began when Lima Company got hit. Sanders' squad was sitting outside of the city during this part of the fighting. When the rest of the battalion arrived in Husaybah, his squad went with the battalion push through the city, block by block. They went from the east end all the way to the west end of Husaybah. Sanders said that squads and platoons had rehearsed this type of movement, but they had not done it on a battalion level before arrival here. After sweeping through Husaybah, the battalion stayed "firm" on a road on the western part of the city. He said that a second sweep through the city the next day, this time from north to south, went "pretty smooth, nothing happened."

When the sweeps were done, Kilo Company returned to Camp Al Qaim, and Lima Company went back to its normal patrols in the city. "I think we got our point across when we swept through them the first time, sir." He added that since then, there have been IED attacks, but no large-scale fighting. He was on Hill 227 for the past few days, and estimated that four IEDs went off within the past 24 hours in the AO.

Sanders described current operations in Kilo Company. "We have a rotation now, Hill 212, it's an OP, we conduct a React patrol into the city either from Sada, Karabilah, to the HK [in Husaybah], we can react to Lima."

It's a central area in the AO, and they can react and go where needed. In the small towns they will do a mounted patrol, then dismount and walk for part of the time.

"We'll link up with Iraqi police in Karabilah, do a joint patrol with them, and basically, just presence, let 'em know we're still here." It's a two-day rotation in the towns, then four days back in the rear at Camp Al Qaim.

Lance Corporal Sanders finished by talking about the difference between being in Iraq last year and this year. He said that down in Karbala it wasn't too dangerous last year, just random fire, and more civil affairs and humanitarian missions. This year, there was more resistance to the Marine presence.

I asked about the average Iraqi that he sees in the town now compared to their arrival in March this year. He said that the locals seem to understand that the Marines are here to help. During a search, if a door gets kicked in, the homeowner will get a payment of about $80 to $100, and if a window is destroyed, it will bring about $50. Also, "You can tell if something's going down in town, there's no kids around, it's, ah, something's about to happen. Yesterday kids were out playing, everybody's out working, all the shops were working, so it's been going pretty good."

Corporal Kristopher Elliot Benson
Section Leader, CAAT Blue Charlie,
Weapons Company, 3/7

Corporal Benson was a member of one of the Combined Anti-Armor Teams that was attached to Kilo Company 3/7 during the April 2004 combat operations in Husaybah. His team also captured an 8mm video camera that provided intelligence on terrorists' activities in the town.

This young Marine graduated from MCRD San Diego in October 2001. When he joined 3/7, he was assigned as an 81mm mortar man.

In addition to CAX (Combined Arms Exercise) training with the battalion, he attended the Defense Language Institute four-week Arabic course to gain some familiarity with the language.

When 3/7 arrived in Iraq in March, Weapons Company created a third section for operations here, and Corporal Benson became a section leader with CAAT platoon. "We came over in separate platoons, we had the Heavy Machine Gun Platoon, Anti-Armor Platoon, and Mortar Platoon. We came together as a Combined Anti Armor Team once we got into Kuwait. And the difference about our CAAT teams now, as opposed to the last time we were here, as the CAAT teams operate: We have the 81s, the mortar men mixed in with them, since we're not using the indirect fire systems here, it gives the CAAT team a dismounted capability that it normally doesn't have."

For about two weeks they did some work-up training in Udari, Kuwait, before convoying up here. The CAAT teams were responsible for providing convoy security for most of 3/7. They stopped in the Karbala area, through Camp Fallujah, and then into the Al Qaim area. On arrival here, he participated in the Left-seat, Right-seat familiarization with the area of operations. The US Army units that were here had tanks and Bradley fighting vehicles, much more heavily armored than a Marine infantry unit.

They began mounted patrols from the Syrian border all the way to the eastern part of the AO. "We've attached CAAT teams to each of the line [infantry] companies, so each CAAT team has a different sector of the AO that they're operating in. The sector that I'm responsible would be the eastern sector, out to Jubayil."

They operate throughout the area, and also provide a QRF for the battalion, convoy escorts, VIP escorts, CASEVAC for ground evacuations, and escort for wrecker vehicles. "A lot of times we get tasked with taking EOD [Explosive Ordnance Disposal] out to an IED site, as well as OPs, VCPs, and raids."

I asked him about the four-week-long Arabic course that he had taken, what level of fluency he was able to develop, and if he has had an opportunity to use these skills. He responded: "Definitely had the opportunity to use it. I would say that the fluency level is pretty minimal. It was a good course. The Iraqi dialect is an unwritten language, so they [the instructors] focused mostly on just speaking it, understanding it. Four weeks to learn it was a very, very short time. But I think most of the people in the course walked away with a familiarity with simple words, that at least helped in a context to kinda understand what somebody's conveying. I think some people probably walked away with a little bit better understanding than others. But we were able to develop cards that help us, kind of a 'cheat card' to ask somebody to open up their [car] trunk or tell them to put their hands up, things like that." He said that it was more for giving commands and interrogation.

Corporal Benson's CAAT section was with several other CAAT sections in the town of Ubaidi on the morning of April 17 when they got the call that fighting had begun in Husaybah.

"We heard about the initial contact with Lima Company, and then about an hour or so later that the fight was still goin' on, and battalion was movin' a large portion of the battalion into the Husaybah area to cordon. Which time we started runnin' VCPs from Ubaidi all the way to Husaybah, to basically screen any [insurgent] reinforcements that might have been coming into the area, and sealing off any escape routes that the insurgents might be usin'. My section went into Husaybah, and secured the LZ Eagle, for the CASEVACs. And I don't know what it was classified as when the birds landed, but just prior to them bein' there, it was a hot LZ. There was firefights all around it. And then we maintained a cordon for the next 48 hours around the city."

His section helped maintain the cordon on April 18 while the line companies did their north-to-south sweep of Husaybah. Since that time, his section has mainly supported Kilo Company operations in the three main built-up areas in their zone.

"I definitely sense a shift since the 17th. I think that was our first major engagement with the enemy, I think they underestimated what our capabilities were ... they hit us, and we hit them back pretty hard. We mobilized very quickly to surround the city, cordoned it off, and I think that sent a message to them. I know a number of the enemy were killed in that engagement. We've begun to see a lot more cooperation I think, from the locals. Just in my interaction with them I know that a lot of 'em look at that April 17th contact, they blame the insurgents for the violence, they understand that our reaction was to their aggression, and not just, an overreaction."

Corporal Benson said that the Marines had started to get more intelligence from local Iraqis, and sense a loss of support for insurgents. He feels that this may be why there has been a decrease in insurgent activity over the past month and a half. There have still been IEDs almost every day, but with limited effect on the Marines. The Marines find a lot of these devices. There has been almost no direct contact with insurgents. Also, he said that VCPs have helped slow the flow of weapons and IEDs into the area.

"We've educated ourselves to the point where we now know what a lot of the components for the IEDs look like, so if they're not bringin' them in as a package, they're bringing them in as separate parts. We can recognize that. Just the other day we found a truckload of cell phones, and the guy driving the truck doesn't know who he's deliverin' it to. It's pretty suspicious. Hopefully that's 45 IEDs that didn't get made."

I then asked Corporal Benson to discuss operations in Iraq last year during the initial invasion. He described it as "night and day" compared to this year. Last year he was in Karbala for four or five months, and the locals wanted them there more, and the people were happy just to see Saddam Hussein gone. There were only a few sporadic fights. This year 3/7 is in a different area, the Army operated differently than the Marines in here. "The enemy contact has been ten-fold compared to the war last year."

In terms of current operations, Benson said that finding IEDs has been more difficult than expected. Sometimes the insurgents are sloppy in burying them, but the ones that have detonated near him, he says he never saw coming. They drove right over them and the enemy hit them with the IEDs. "We actually caught a guy who had a videotape of one of our vehicles getting hit with an IED. And that's kinda snowballed into more intelligence on forces operating in that area. It's netted a few of the terrorists."

He added that it was remarkable to see both sides of an IED attack on them—they experienced the explosion, and then they saw the explosion from the triggerman's view.

I then asked, "How did you find this guy's videotape?" Corporal Benson replied: "We were running a VCP, it was actually one of the other sections, CAAT Red was running a VCP, noticed a vehicle that was approaching them, stop, turned around, obviously didn't want to go through the VCP. They gave chase to them, the guy ditched his car, took off runnin'. Kinda cop style. And when they searched his car, found a Super 8 video camera, with an IED [recorded] on it. And in the trunk of his car they found eight HIND rockets. So, there's 57mm helicopter rockets that they'd built a homemade rocket launcher out of, and fired with a 9-volt battery. He had videotaped one of his friend's houses, and his father's house, and just by walking through the city where his car was confiscated, we were able to locate the two houses he had videotaped and arrested the people there. And through their confessions, kinda givin' up some more people. That's kinda how the intelligence circle works, I guess. We haven't found him yet, we haven't found the makers of the IEDs, but we think we know who they are and we're looking for them."

He said that the job here was complicated and difficult, trying to gain the trust of the local population while fighting insurgents. There are terrorists coming from outside Iraq in addition to local fighters. "A lot of the Marines are focused on what they're doing."

The Marines are professional, and are doing their jobs. He doesn't feel that the Marines blame local individuals for the actions against them. "The war is bigger than Iraq."

Captain Bradford Wilson Tippett
Commanding Officer, India Company, 3/7

"Our Marines train hard and well." Tippett's India Company Marines were tasked with providing internal and external force protection at Camp Al Qaim. India was also involved in liaison with local Iraqi Civil Defense Corps units.

Captain Tippett entered the Marine Corps through the PLC program, and was commissioned in December 1995. He served as a rifle platoon commander for 23 months with 2/2. He then served at MCRD, Parris Island for 38 "long" months, completed EWS at Quantico, and arrived at 3/7 in August 2003.

After a period of block leave for the Marines in 3/7, he began what he called a traditional block-training program to prepare for deployment to Okinawa. But in October 2003, he began receiving indications that the battalion might be returning to Iraq sometime in 2004. He then started to focus on company-level skills that his Marines would need. Both the division and regiment mandated training that would be needed for SASO in Iraq. "That occupied a large portion of our time, both in December and January, prior to our deployment.

"I was on the first wave goin' out. My company followed me afterwards." He and an NCO came to Kuwait, Captain Tippett's first time in Theater. "We settled into Camp Udari pretty quickly." There he began preparations for operations at Camp Al Qaim, and also planning the main convoy up into Iraq from Kuwait. Plans had to be constantly updated as conditions warranted. One item was the fact that the Marines would be replacing the U.S. Army's 1st of the 3rd Mechanized Battalion. They have much more armor than a Marine battalion, and operate very differently than a Marine infantry battalion. "Their attitudes, mentality, and resources were completely different from what we fell in on with our gear and capabilities." Captain Tippett said that where the Army set a tank, he set a Marine with an M16. It's just a different way of operating.

He flew from Udari to Al Assad, Iraq, then to Camp Al Qaim, arriving around February 11, 2004. The Army did share lots of information about the AO, which has helped.

India Company's main mission on arrival at this camp was to provide security for the camp itself, including a nine-kilometer area around the camp. Shortly before the Marines arrived at Camp Al Qaim, the Army received a hit from a 122mm rocket, so the Marines determined to keep a 24-hour presence in the area around the camp. "We had four Humvees to operate out there on squad-size patrols, patrolling both north and south, east and west of the city area." He said that this was a pretty effective way to discourage indirect fire, as they only received two more indirect fire hits on the camp. The last 122mm rocket fired at the camp was from about 15 kilometers away, from north of the river, showing that the insurgents also adapt to the tactics of the Marines' patrolling.

He then spoke about another task for his company: "The other mission we had assigned to us was to train and equip and supervise the ICDC. We arrived in theater; we quickly came to the realization that the ICDC was the probably most mature security organization in the zone." The U.S. Army MPs that were here had established an IP (Iraqi Police) training academy here. Captain Tippett and his first sergeant worked with Civil Affairs Marines to help provide the equipment, everything from boots and uniforms to administering pay for the training of the local police. They have already trained about 100 Iraqi recruits, and have another training class ongoing. "I focused a lot of attention on that, and had my XO manage a lot of the daily patrols."

Captain Tippett assigned Staff Sergeant Lopez as his force protection platoon commander. He also has augments from H&S (Headquarters and Service) Company 3/7 and H&S Company LAR battalion to help man posts at the camp and provide needed manpower to meet his security requirements. In addition to the security outside the camp, he is also tasked with providing internal camp security, as there are local Iraqis who work inside the camp. They provide services such as waste disposal, water trucks, and there are also contractors and visitors who have business on the camp. "We've implemented a badge system, and search them pretty well at a control point."

He said that the chances of a ground assault against the camp are pretty low, given the limited resources available to insurgents, and the location of this camp in the middle of a desert. However, there is a building on the northern side of the train tracks that the U.S. Army had to turn over to the Iraqis for use as a civilian train terminal. This building is not yet active, but a passenger rail car from Baghdad comes through twice a day. Captain Tippett has installed an outpost on top of this building to keep an eye on activities there.

The Army had allowed several small Iraqi businesses to operate on the camp, including a small store and a coffee shop, right across from the COC. After the relief in place, these shops were moved down a hill, away from the COC.

Captain Tippett's company is responsible for searching for IEDs on the two ASRs (alternate supply roads) in his zone. They have not found any IEDs to date, but have found "a pretty fair amount of UXO [unexploded ordnance] in my zone." His patrols go out for 48-hour operations.

I asked him to explain how he rotates his platoons to keep them fresh.

"I have a cycle that works in this manner: I'll have one platoon that is out on a 48-hour operation, the platoon that is in the chute behind them is conducting company react, they're on standby to respond to different things, and or augment the battalion as necessary. Their chief responsibility as the reaction force for the company is to respond in my zone. That platoon rotates a squad through so a squad's on 'ready five' and the platoon is on 'ready thirty'."

That means that the platoon can respond in 30 minutes in the company's zone.

"The other platoon that comes back from the 48-hour patrols goes into a rest day, that second day in the 48-hour rotation day is a training day, that they conduct training and maintenance."

He works this schedule with three of his platoons, while his 4th Platoon has been assigned to work in Husaybah. Also, a platoon from Lima Company gets sent to his company every 15 days, and Captain Tippett allows them to rest and refit, as well as provide manpower for guard duties when needed.

Around April 17–18, Captain Tippett had one of his platoons (1st Platoon) on battalion QRF. "They were deployed within about four hours of the first contact beginning. They picked up and conducted operations in Husaybah under the battalion commander, chiefly. They conducted several missions in Husaybah. I had another platoon [Weapons Platoon] that was my reaction force. We sent them to establish a traffic control point at checkpoint Sierra Two." Battalion then made the decision to deploy Weapons Company into Husaybah, and one of India Company's platoons was attached. So it wound up that two of Captain Tippett's platoons were in the thick of the action in Husaybah that day. He had one platoon at the camp with about 37 Marines total. They did not see any small arms fire at the camp that night, but did see some pyrotechnic signaling in the distance.

His platoon with Weapons Company provided security at LZ Eagle at a soccer field in the eastern end of Husaybah that night. His 1st Platoon, which was the QRF, linked up with some units from Kilo Company and got involved in some firefights with the enemy, and also conducted a medevac for a Kilo Company platoon in southeast Husaybah. Captain Tippett estimated that these Marines of his had been deployed for about 26 hours, came back and got about three hours of sleep, and then went back out again to pick up detainees and remain on the QRF mission. "Like everyone else, we surged what we had and Marines stayed on post [for about 72 hours]."

"I'm surprised, but never cease to be amazed by their resilience and their ability to keep on goin' with regards to how long they've been operatin' for. They prove themselves across the board from the task force to the Marines on camp to the ones out forward fighting in Husaybah. They all did a helluva job."

I asked how he keeps going with all of this going on. He said that his XO is fully capable of operating the company. They have worked out a rotation so that there is a good rest cycle. The XO knew that Captain Tippett would be the one to go out when the company made contact with the enemy, and he worked longer hours in the COC to allow the captain to be rested for movement.

His first sergeant, First Sergeant Breeze, has been a tremendous asset to Captain Tippett. Breeze is a Recon Marine and works well to prepare the Marines for contact with the enemy.

In the most recent weeks, there has been a slight increase in enemy contact. But his company's operations do not surge unless there is major contact. The constant coverage that India Company provides in the area discourages enemy activity close to the camp.

To wrap up the interview, Tippett said, "The Marines train hard and train well. No matter how experienced, they have done a hell of a job. When the Marines provide a safe haven on the camp for the other Marines in the area, they are doing their job well."

Staff Sergeant Alexander Anthony Carlson
Platoon Sergeant, 3rd Platoon, India Company 3/7

"I'm impressed by how the Marines deal with operations. The corporals and lance corporals are doing a lot." This platoon sergeant's Marines were tasked with round-the-clock security operations throughout the Al Qaim area.

Staff Sergeant Carlson joined the Marine Corps in March 1993 and did his recruit training at MCRD San Diego. He served with 2/3 in Hawaii, then with 1st FAST (Fleet Anti-Terrorism Security Team) Company at Norfolk, Virginia. I first met him at San Diego, California in the summer of 2000 when I taught him in a Western Civilization course at the MECEP program. He completed OCS at Quantico in 2001, but did not receive his officer's commission, as he did not complete his college course work within the time limit. So he returned to the Fleet as a staff sergeant with Weapons Company, 3/7. In October 2002, he was involved with the workup to go to OIF I. He served as a section leader with 81mm mortars, and once they crossed the Line of Departure, they moved to Karbala.

3/7 redeployed to OIF II on Valentine's Day, 2004, moving through Camp Udari, Kuwait. Carlson said that there was a lot of "friction" within the company prior to the deployment, but the focus became clear once they arrived in Kuwait. They were able to do some cross training prior to the convoy into Iraq at the beginning of March. It took four days of convoy movement to move up to Al Assad, then the company traveled to Al Qaim via CH 53s.

Once at Al Qaim, "We did a little Left-seat, Right-seat. We went on, First [Sergeant] and I went on two patrols with the Army, one on the right seat, one on the left seat. It seemed like a lot of complacency." I asked, "Among the Army?" Carlson said, "Yes, not to really judge the tactics, but after 14 months, it was good to share a lot of the TTPs that they used with mines and IEDs. We didn't see that last time down in Karbala. And if we did, it was a flash in the pan."

Staff Sergeant Carlson had never seen an up-armored Humvee here when he was in Iraq last year, but the Army now had many of them.

He said that Camp Al Qaim was well set-up security-wise. The Army personnel were happy to be leaving, and were generous in gear that they left behind, like M16 magazines, and maps. Once the Army units left, India Company began its 24-hour patrolling effort: "One platoon would go out, next platoon would be on react, the platoon getting ready to go out would be on react, and the platoon that just came back in would be on a rest day." It was a three-day cycle for all of the platoons in the company.

Now that the company was on a six-day cycle, I asked about the organizing he has to do as a platoon sergeant. "At any given time I have a couple of Marines tasked out to mess hall duty, detainee center, and guard duty. Just recently returned from patrol so this is the second day of my rest period. I have numbers due around 5:30 so I'm up around 4:45, numbers in. We have about a 6:30 reveille, depending on if the guys were up late. If the guys were up later, got called on a React, we let 'em sleep late. We try not to make too many rules for 'em, but they get up around 6:30."

The Marines will do some PT or the gym before it gets too hot. On the day of rest he'll get them one little class (with topics such as optics on the new gun sights, or heavy weapons) to keep them proactive in everything they are doing, and then let them relax as they want. Staff Sergeant Carlson said that each platoon now has about a dozen ACOGs (enhanced M16 sights). On the React day, he breaks it into time cycles for each squad in the platoon. "That react is called out for any local disturbance, whether it be sheep herders [who] appear to be observing the camp, anything locally."

During the React days, he issues the Op (Operating) Order for the patrols to the squad leaders, and they can work on their map overlays to prepare for the patrols.

"We're a little bit luckier, since it's a little bit less of a threat it seems, than would be inside the cities, and these guys have time to be working on basic infantry skills. The next day they issue their order to their fire team leaders and squads. We usually do a confirmation briefing the night before, or the morning of, they step off on patrol. Sometime between 0900 and 1100 we do a relief in place. We have three squads, so we do three different patrols. One is always at our Retrans site, one is foot-mobile, one is vehicle-mounted on four Humvees. SOP [standard operating procedure] right now is four Humvees when we travel around the area. Basically, it's a mine threat for a Humvee. And then we rotate every 16 hours out there so that someone's not out there baking at the Retrans site. Forty-eight hours seems to be going well right now, we haven't experienced any heat casualties."

Every platoon has had some type of contact during this deployment. "Marines are very alert," Staff Sergeant Carlson said. He added that the Kevlars (helmets) stay on.

When the fighting happened in mid-April in Husaybah, his Marines were active. One of his squads on react wound up spending the night in Husaybah, as part of the security for LZ Eagle near the soccer field in the eastern part of the city. The platoon still had the camp security mission. Squads have been tasked with leading patrols into Karabilah, Ubaidi, and Husaybah. Staff Sergeant Carlson himself tries to stay with the mobile squad a lot. The local curfew is now from 2300 until 0400, and he is involved with controlling the traffic. When back at camp, he stands watch every third day. "We do a pretty good job of rotating; I don't think anybody's getting overworked."

I asked him to detail some of the differences between last year and this year. Last year he was in charge of a section of 81mm mortars, with a lot of autonomy. He let corporals lead convoys on their own. Now, as a platoon sergeant, he is more involved in planning. Last year there was not as much direct fire at him or his Marines. There has been more fire at his Marines, both direct and indirect at different times. He enjoys watching the young Marines grow as leaders this year. He said that it's not like last time, with the Iraqi Army running from superior air power and ground fire. The enemy this year is smart, with constantly evolving tactics. His Marines are not resting on their laurels, but are working hard out there every day. "I think the guys are workin' twice as hard as last time."

There is not as much interaction with Iraqi civilians as there was last time. Last year he was in meetings at Karbala with local leaders, but this year he has less contact with the civilians in Husaybah.

In conclusion Staff Sergeant Carlson said: "I'm impressed with how these Marines had to deal with it. You know, bein' a platoon sergeant, havin' a little experience, it's easy for me. I think I, I'm expected to think outside of the box, and come up with these ideas, and try to be the witty one, go into battle. But the small unit leaders, unlike OIF I [when it seemed so easy] … it's all the corporals and the sergeants. I was never this good, I think. These guys have stepped up. They've run the whole battle."

Gunnery Sergeant Brian Wayne Eyestone
Platoon Sergeant, 5th Platoon, 1st Force Recon Company

Gunny Eyestone provided a real good explanation of how a recon platoon has reinforced a Marine infantry battalion operating in western Iraq. His Marines were actively involved in both of the battalion sweeps through Husaybah on April 17 and 18, as well as continuing security actions throughout the region.

Gunnery Sergeant Eyestone entered the Corps in June 1990. After his basic training and SOI (School of Infantry), he was accepted into 1st Force Recon Company, and served there until 1996. He served on Embassy duty for two and a half years before returning to Force Recon in 1999.

To get ready for this deployment he said, "The biggest hurdle was figuring out just who was going and getting them all together into the platoon, and then how late we found out, kinda cramming some of our training in. We went through a field shooting package into more of a precision shooting package of sorts." They did vehicle patrolling, vehicle raids, some urban sniping training, some rescue and search training, communications, combat trauma training, and patrolling. "We deployed a week after the actual regiment did." This was in February 2004. "We never trained with 3/7 at all until we got here."

Fortunately, his platoon commander had come from 3/7, and was with 3/7 during OIF I. This made the attachment much smoother for the Recon Marines. Gunny Eyestone says that normally the platoon would support a MEU (Marine Expeditionary Unit), and do a six-month workup on its own, and six months working with the MEU prior to deployment. The Recon platoon did not actually "marry up" with 3/7 until they met up with them at Al Assad.

Initially, 3/7 was looking to have the Recon Marines participate in raids, provide snipers, and go after HVTs (high-value targets, or individuals of interest) as part of SASO operations.

"It was actually not too long after we were here we actually did our first raid. They had a list of people that they had information on, and only some had been solidified by more than one source. So we ended up doin' a raid on two houses at the same time, where it was us and a unit from 3/7 to help set up the cordon."

After that they hooked up with Lima Company, and sent four to five Marines at a time to go out on the foot-mobile patrols to get a feel for the area, and do urban patrols and sniper ops. They also rode along with CAAT vehicles to learn the area. Then they went out to an area north of Husaybah, which Eyestone described as a shelf that overlooks the whole valley.

Around April 17, in Husaybah, three teams from the Recon platoon were with different companies in 3/7. "We began the 17th at Market Street in Husaybah," Eyestone said. They helped to set up a security line around the battalion headquarters element, while "Blade" (Lieutenant Colonel Lopez's call sign) was talking by radio to the Lima Company XO. They were about one block east of the Baath Party headquarters, and began taking some small arms fire from people in alleyways. The element that he was with was mounted on three vehicles with weapons on them, about 17 Marines altogether. As they prepared to begin the sweep westward into the city, he could see guys walking around in the city of Husaybah, seemingly oblivious to the Marines. "It almost appeared that every time we saw a guy cross a road, there was a kid with him."

When they went into the city, they began moving slowly. Some Marines were mounted and some on foot near the Humvees. Then, "Our platoon started takin' fire from a building, we started returning fire, and it was, the building that was between our street and the street to the south, which was our other route that Recon platoon was on, and they started openin' up on it. There was people on a third-story building, where basically all you could see was barrels coming out of the windows, and they were shootin' down on us."

His Marines returned and began to formulate a plan to go into the building. They then went into three buildings in a compound there. To clear the first building, they crossed the street, and knocked down the door, "We were gonna throw a frag [fragmentation grenade] to clear the first building, but it was a good thing we didn't, because as we went in, there was a family there. So, it was our platoon commander who had the grenade at the time, he held onto it, went to an area with nobody in it, and threw it into this one room and got rid of the grenade." (I know from my own training that once a grenade pin has been pulled out from the "spoon" of the grenade, as it had been here, the grenade is armed and dangerous and needs to be disposed of quickly if not used for its intended purpose.)

To get into the next building in the compound, the Marines had to go back outside of the first building, because the second building had barred windows and no access from the first. His Marines started clearing in through this second building where the insurgents were located.

"Once we started clearing the buildings, the shooting out onto the street had stopped. So, we went in. The first floor was clear. We found some families on the second floor that had three males in there. The way they were, and the way they acted, they didn't act like they mighta been any bad guys. They were all huddling, together with their families."

Gunnery Sergeant Eyestone sent these Iraqis out of the building to the other building to get them out of harm's way. "Then we cleared the third floor, which was where the guys who were shooting at us were." The only thing that was found was some brass (bullet shell casings) and some evidence of people having been squatters there (cooking utensils, etc.). Outside of the building were rooftops of other buildings where the insurgents could have jumped to get away. Since 3/7 was continuing the sweep, the platoon could not stay in the area and search for the shooters.

The sweep continued with no major shooting at them.

Near a gas station near the West End Road, along Market, they set up and waited for the battalion to complete the sweep. There was some sporadic firing at their position, but once teams of Marines were sent up onto the tops of some buildings nearby, the shooting stopped.

"We held that position until it got dark and then ourselves and the OGA [Other Government Agency] guys moved onto Market. Basically the plan from there was to set up on Market and set up a perimeter around the whole city and not let anything in or out."

They would wait until morning for any further actions. "We went onto the north side of Trash Road, set up our vehicles." His platoon set up and tied in with an adjacent platoon. "You could see the Cobras firing their rockets and guns down south of Husaybah." There were some other firefights in the city, but not near his platoon.

After midnight, things quieted down. Later that night, some Intel was received that was begun by a phone call. They went into a school building on this tip, but did not find anything and pulled back to their staging area. They then went into the Lima Company compound, picked up one of their Recon teams, and then returned to Camp Al Qaim.

Since then, his platoon has provided VCPs, both planned and "snap", acted as a React force at times, been with Kilo Company to a water treatment plant at Karabilah and provided OPs and sniper overwatch there. The longest break between missions has been 36 hours. "We've been keeping' pretty busy." While at a Kilo Company Firm Base, they received incoming fire, and the Kilo Company Reaction force moved quickly into the city to look for the shooters. Gunnery Sergeant Eyestone's platoon commander offered to put his Marines to whatever uses the rifle company commander wanted. They were sent outside the protective berms at the base to check out a taxi that had been shot at when it failed to stop approaching the base. This taxi matched the description of VBIEDs (vehicle-borne improvised explosive devices) that the battalion had been warning about, and the driver had climbed out and tried to run away after the vehicle was hit by small arms fire.

As they cautiously approached the taxi, they saw a hand waving from it. Three Marines were sent to see who this survivor was. The hand was waving what appeared to be an ID card. He appeared wounded, and the three Marines got to the man and checked out his ID card. The Marines moved the man to a safe area and called for a Corpsman. Iraqi police came and took both the wounded man and the dead man from the vehicle to the hospital. "We never went into the trunk of the car, because we thought if there was an IED in it, someone might trigger it." His Marines later pulled back into the Firm Base.

Most recently they went north of the Euphrates river on the bluffs, with one team clandestinely placed close to the Syrian border. Around the time this team was pulled out, there was some cross-border shooting between Iraqi border guards and Syrian border guards.

The Recon Marines have participated in many sweeps in the battalion's AO. The platoon has been hit by IEDs four times. Once, on a foot patrol to set up an OP at the Baath Party Headquarters, there was a big boom, and a wall was blown up. "One guy was like, 'Hey, I think I've been hit'." The hit Marine, Corporal Ross, was next to Gunnery Sergeant Eyestone. He had some minor wounds, but also a sucking chest wound 'through and through.' The pieces missed all of his protective gear to cause these wounds. Within less than 15 minutes, CAAT came and grabbed Ross. The Corpsman sealed up the wound and within 35 minutes, Ross was back at the FRSS at Al Qaim. In less than 20 hours, Ross was in Germany, and in two to three days was at Bethesda Naval Hospital in the States.

Another time around the 17th, two IEDs went off at once and two of Eyestone's Marines got shrapnel wounds. In a patrol north of the river, one Humvee hit a land mine—it was the last vehicle in a four-vehicle patrol. Then another Humvee in the patrol hit a mine when it drove off the road after the first explosion. No one was seriously hurt. Their vehicles have been slowly getting up-armored. At first they had metal half doors, and the several "high back" Humvees had metal plates in the back area where Marines rode. And about a week ago, a fourth IED hit a vehicle. They were headed up towards the bluff that overlooks the river, Gunny Eyestone explained.

"Again, I was in one of the last vehicles in our group, right after the "S" turn, two vehicles got hit by IEDs simultaneously, near simultaneously. One went off in front of the lead vehicle, didn't really throw too much back at 'em, and the other one went off right next to the second vehicle. That second vehicle, all it received was like explosives that threw up clouds and dirt. It was like a fireball kinda went up."

The Marines had recently installed three-quarter armored doors with ballistic windshields on their Humvees, and Gunny Eyestone credits them with saving some lives that day. The Marines in the second vehicle received no injuries, but the shrapnel that was shot forward towards the first vehicle caused three routine casualties there. Two of these Marines were peppered with small cuts, but a third Marine had the SAPI plates of his flak jacket to thank for saving his life. One piece of shrapnel that was stopped was the size of a quarter, and the Kevlar material in the vest stopped another nickel-size piece. The shrapnel caused huge welts, but no cuts on the Marine. "Obviously, shook him up a little bit," said Eyestone.

I asked him about how his newer Marines are doing. He estimated that about 75 percent of his Marines were here last year for OIF I. He said that everyone performs well. They have been professional and restrained, even during the height of the fighting in mid-April.

He said that getting "blown up," i.e., hit by an IED, makes the situation real. Also, his living quarters are near the FRSS at the camp, and when the helos come in people always wonder who has been hit. Gunnery Sergeant Eyestone is obviously satisfied and proud of the job his Marines have been doing over here.

Corporal Michael Thomas Phillips
Combat Engineer, 1st Combat Engineer Battalion,
attached to 3/7

A veteran of OIF-1, he found this deployment to have more threats from IEDs and mortar fire. Combat Engineer Marines helped to build barriers, sweep for mines, fortify Camp Husaybah, and do urban demolition during combat operations.

Corporal Phillips entered the Marine Corps in April 2001. After training he joined the Fleet in November that year. His first deployment was in OIF I; he arrived in Kuwait in February 2003 and then "went to war" with 3/7. He said that he didn't see as much as some Marines did. He helped clear minefields, did some urban demolitions, blowing doors and locks off, and helping the grunts clear the buildings. He then went with 3/7 to Karbala in southern Iraq where they did stabilization operations. He spent two or three months blowing up UXO and returned with 3/7 in September 2003. "We got shot at I think twice, the whole time we were at Karbala."

A couple of months after returning to the States, they got word that they'd be going back to Iraq. He was only home about five months or so before he redeployed to Iraq. "It's what we do as Marines," he said.

I asked how the Engineers were trained when they went to March Air Force Base. He responded, "As Engineers attached out to a grunt battalion, we'll get attached out to companies, and breaks it down even further, we'll take a fire team into a squad. And a platoon'll get attached out to a company. We'll go. We'll help them build their Firm Base. We'll do general engineering. We'll go out on patrols. If they need a door blown, we have demolition. We have a breacher's kit, where we have bolt cutters, things like that."

He arrived in Kuwait at about the same time he did the year before. "We spent about two weeks there, getting gear ready, getting ourselves ready." Then they convoyed up to Camp Al Qaim. Within another fortnight, engineer teams were sent out to the rifle companies. His team went to help with constructing HESCO barriers and towers on the Firm Base in Husaybah. This is part of the Engineers' area of expertise, but

Corporal Phillips said that in his three years in the Corps, he normally was involved in things like mine clearing and blowing open doors and walls. "First three weeks we were up there, we got hit by mortars every day. And then it kind of slowed down a little bit. And gave us a little time to actually get out and build the things we needed to build and fortify the base."

He said that when Marines work in the Division, they get into the infantryman's mindset, working with ground units, helping with urban demolition and working with mine detectors. But they also have training in construction.

He said, "We've done a lot of that out here, as far as urban demolitions. From maybe blowing a door, you might have to blow a door to get into a car, it just depends."

"I've blown a bunch of stuff like that here, from things like padlocks. You put maybe a quarter stick of C4, or a doughnut charge. And all that is, is a bunch of det cord that's wrapped, and you put it on the lock, and you'll blow it. We've done a lot of that over here." He said that a lot of gates around houses are locked, and a lot of doors have been on places where they've gone in and found "lots of stuff" in the way of weapons and ammunition. He has even blown up small caches of mortar rounds, something that is usually the job of EOD, because the EOD Marines are so busy and the ammo that was found needed to be destroyed.

I asked him about IEDs, and he replied: "I actually got hit by an IED about a month ago. I got a piece of frag in my neck. We [Engineers] don't really mess with IEDs, that's really an EOD thing." Corporal Phillips said that IEDs were completely different from the land mines that they were used to working with. The Engineers don't really want to touch the IEDs at all. Infantrymen will mark the IED and have EOD come out to demolish the explosive devices. "IEDs aren't fun, I been around probably two or three of them when they went off, and the one that I got hit by, I was about 15 yards away from it." He added, "We had just got out of a vehicle on a raid. It was probably a couple of weeks after the happenings up in Husaybah. We're doin' a raid on a suspected meeting place, bomb making place. My platoon had got attached out to the grunt platoon that was out there." He said that it was a pretty big operation.

"There was probably two or three 7-tons [trucks] full of Marines, and what we were doin', as Engineers we're pretty much supporting the grunts." The infantry had gone on ahead, and some of the other Marines stayed with the vehicles and were beginning to move them to a more secure site. "We were all takin' cover along the side of the road, next thing I know I see a large flash of light. It was one of my Marines, he was directly in front of me, he fell right in front of me, I thought he had gotten killed. He went down real fast. And I noticed a lot of other Marines were just laying around, too. I was kinda in shell shock at first. It was kinda a concussion."

He said that the IED was determined to be made from a 155mm artillery round that exploded. "We were lucky. If they woulda set it off probably a minute before that, when we had just got there, it woulda been a lot worse. Nobody got killed that day." At the time it happened, Corporal Phillips didn't realize that he had been hit because he was busy getting his Marines up and into safety.

The past few weeks have been quiet for him and his Marines. "It's pretty quiet here [at Camp Al Qaim]." The chow is better and the quarters are air-conditioned. Also, about half of his platoon is new, as well as the platoon commander and platoon sergeant.

There are many contrasts between last year and this year in Iraq. He was in Karbala then, and it was peaceful and quiet, the people there liked them. This year, there is a constant IED threat, along with a threat of being mortared. It's more of a combat-type environment. "You have to be a lot more aware."

Staff Sergeant Ronnie Lee King
Platoon Sergeant, MP Platoon, Charlie Company, attached to 3/7

A Marine reservist called to active duty in 2003, Staff Sergeant King was now on second combat deployment. He explained how the Military Police were being used in the Al Qaim area, some in what might be considered traditional MP missions, and also a new mission of training local Iraqi police.

Staff Sergeant King originally served on active duty from 1986 to 1990, and was an accountant (MOS 3451). He did a lateral move, and served as an Embassy guard for his last two and a half years on active duty. He then went to college and obtained his degree, and was in and out of the Reserves twice, picking up the Military Police MOS in 1994. In March 2003, his reserve Military Police unit was activated for OIF I. They returned to the US in October 2003, and the night of the unit's Marine Corps Birthday Ball, when everyone was getting off active duty, they learned that they would be kept on active duty and returned to Iraq to support OIF II.

In December, they did the MOUT training package, then in January 2004 reported to 29 Palms and were attached as a company to 3/7. The company was split up: King's platoon was attached to 3/7, another platoon to 2/7, and a third platoon attached to RCT1. "We are running an Iraqi police training package, 2nd Platoon is running, or trying to get into that." The 3rd Platoon (with RCT1) was running a prison for detainees in the Fallujah area and is currently doing EOD escorts and escort security.

When the MPs reported to 29 Palms, they did not have a lot of their gear, as it had not come back from Iraq last year. To train, they needed to borrow gear from other Marine units. They arrived in Kuwait in mid-February, spent about two weeks there, and the first mission was as the escort elements for 3/7's convoys from Kuwait up to Camp Al Qaim. Once at the camp, they set up an Iraqi Police Academy, run by half of the MP Platoon. The other half of the platoon runs operations out in town (Husaybah). "We go out in town and we'll spend about four days in a police station, once we get enough recruits, set up all the administrative, timekeeping, basic." They were now covering their second police station. "Making sure the police are properly wearing their uniforms, showing up for work, and find out what's going on in the town."

The MPs are an FSSG (Force Service Support Group) unit, and normally their role is rear-area security, handling enemy prisoners of war, battlefield circulation and control, and MSR security. They did these things during OIF I, but this year have taken on new missions. They go out into town by themselves, observe what is going on there, watch for IEDs, etc., but their main mission now is training the Iraqi policemen.

I asked him what have been the challenges in training these local police. He responded: "The biggest challenge has been the fact that the Iraqi mindset on how they work, their work ethic. For example, an Iraqi policeman will work 12 hours one day and be off. So they are literally working six months a year. They call in sick, any type of family illness or sickness, or family issue they call off work."

It's not like the American work ethic in showing up for work. Staff Sergeant King said that there are a lot of circumstances which prevent an Iraqi from giving a full workweek. It's a very tribal-oriented society, and he gave me an example of the problems this sometimes causes: Say there was a young, ambitious, police academy graduate who the Marines felt should be promoted to an officer position. If it did not sit well with a tribe, the promotion would not happen. In one case where this happened, the battalion staff spoke with the mayor to smooth things over to get the promotion for a young Iraqi policeman.

With the Iraqi police training, "You don't just say 'this is gonna happen,' there are many rings you have to go through to get anything done." King explained that the Iraqi police don't understand basic concepts such as fortifying a position, standing a post, keeping a helmet and flak jacket on, going out and walking around on patrol, and so forth. When the MPs first arrived, the local police would show up for work, drink chai tea, and never leave the police station. Now they are wearing their uniforms and going on patrol every day.

King feels that any success that his Marines have had in working with the local police chief, officials and the mayor comes because his MPs have lived and worked at two of the police stations for four days at a time. From what he understood, there was no attempt when the Army was here to set up any kind of police training academy. The

Army was sending Iraqi officers and police recruits to the Ramadi area. The MPs have set up an academy that runs for three weeks here at Camp Al Qaim, with emphasis on morality issues, since in prior years, the police in Iraq were corrupt and feared by the people. "They were the people that the public saw as the perpetrators, I believe, of the old regime."

He said that quite a few of the senior police were in the old force. There have been three police classes to date; the first was made up of mostly former police, and the other classes have been new recruits with no police background. Staff Sergeant King said that the newer recruits are highly motivated: "You can tell a huge difference, especially when the grunts come out to start doing the joint patrols with Iraqi police. The motivation, dedication to duty, that the new recruits have compared to the old policemen."

I then asked about the performance of the Iraqi Police during the April fighting in Husaybah. He said that the IPs did not appear with the lockdown and curfew. The first police academy had not yet been completed.

Currently, the main goal is to get the local security forces out and doing patrols. Staff Sergeant King said that on one of the first joint patrols with the Marines, an older Iraqi woman came up and hugged one of the Iraqi policemen with the Marines.

He felt that from the time the war ended through the time that the Army was here, very little was done to build up the local Iraqi security forces, and that the time of the Marines here has been short. There is not much time before his unit will return to the States. He said, "To get more officers on the street, we're hopin' to get another class outta here in a couple weeks. We may get one more class done before July 1st, we have not yet heard what our role is gonna be afterwards." He felt that the current program of local training should have been started right after the Army got here last year. There has been some tension between the "old guard" on the police force and the new police.

To set up the police training academy, he said that each platoon received an extra Staff NCO. In his platoon's case, Gunnery Sergeant

Roberto set up the basic training curriculum. Gunny Roberto is the Reserve unit's I&I Training Chief. Roberto set up the basic SOP, and had four of the MP Marines (who are college graduates) work up the training curriculum. One of these reserve Marines was in law school! Over the sessions of the school, several Iraqis have now become instructors, with a plan for them to take over more of the instruction at the academy.

Between each session of the police academy there is a one-week gap, where admin and background checks, a physical fitness test, medical screening and reading and writing tests will screen an incoming class of police recruits.

The other half of the MP platoon, the "operational" half, will go out into a town and meet with the local police chief and set up a basic work schedule, assign posts, deal with force protection issues for the police station, and coordinate a patrol schedule with a company of Marines assigned to the area. They ensure that the IPs show up for work, and in the proper uniform, micromanaging every little thing to establish the importance of the details in police work. They also are trying to identify IPs who may be potential leaders and can be promoted to more senior positions. Staff Sergeant King would like to see these police officers return to the academy perhaps once a month for some refresher training. The goal is to train 700 local police for the area. The looming date of Iraqi sovereignty (scheduled for July 1) is a concern of his.

When the current deployment ends in September, the MP platoon is scheduled to return to 29 Palms, then return to their own reserve center, and finally get demobilized. Their orders say March 2005 is their demobilization date, but there is the potential for heavy demand for military policemen in the near future here in Iraq.

"My platoon, I literally have three Marines with me now, who their first drill weekend, was about four days before they got activated. Most of my platoon is young. Over half the platoon are in college. I have a young man going back now who has already completed OCS, and is in his last year of school. I got a kid who's already finished one year of law school. Several of us have college degrees."

"For me, it's easy, because I'm already established. I have a job. I have a house." A majority of his platoon are kids who are missing out on college. They have done almost two years of active duty between initial training and then will have a year on active duty. Once demobilized, they will probably get 60 to 90 days off from Reserve training, and then probably go back into a training cycle. However, the rumors persist about the need for a heavy MP presence in OIF.

Staff Sergeant King is proud of the job his young reservists are doing here. "They do not know us as reservists. The majority of the staff we come across are surprised to find that we are reservists." He said that the Marines he has with him are very mature.

Lance Corporal Jerad Duane Allen
Military Policeman, 2nd Platoon, Charlie Company MP, attached to 3/7

On arrival at Camp Al Qaim, his military police platoon was first assigned as a vehicle mounted provisional rifle platoon. Soon they would help establish a local police academy. On April 17, Lance Corporal Allen was part of 3/7's reaction force that punched into Husaybah and took part in 24 hours of fighting.

"I joined the Marine Corps in June, 2002." Although a reservist, Allen spent his first seven months in the Marines on active duty, as he chose to go from recruit training right through his military police school.

"As soon as I came back from MP school, I started going to drill, just like normal, and I got almost a quarter of school in, Ohio State goes in quarters. And right before finals is when we got activated for the first time. So I think I've had four drills total, four months of reserve life before they got me back on active duty."

I asked how his school treated that, as he had not yet completed a full academic quarter. He responded that as he had all A's in most of his classes, most of his professors said that they would give him the grades he had when he left school. Some courses were listed as incomplete, and he hopes to complete them when he is demobilized. He wasn't sure if he would have to pay to complete these courses, but said that he had plenty of money to pay for it now. Of his savings, he said, "There's nothin' else to spend it on," while deployed here in Iraq. "Maybe some extra beef jerky!"

Allen and his fellow Marines served last year for OIF I, and learned that they would be extended on active duty the night of the Marine Corps Ball, in November 2003. They had not yet been demobilized from active duty. He said that, "Most of the guys took it pretty hard. Personally, I took it real hard." (The Ball was at a hotel next to Wright-Patterson Air Force Base, where the unit drills.)

They went to 29 Palms and went through training under 1st Battalion, 7th Marines (1/7). At first they were training for what was supposed to be a relatively benign situation in Iraq, but while at 29 Palms they learned that the environment was more hostile than previously thought.

Lance Corporal Allen traveled to Kuwait, and arrived in Iraq on March 1, 2004. "We moved across the border, it was a big convoy." They knew the roads because they had run so many convoys on the last deployment here. They traveled north up Route Tampa, instead of Route Jackson. Tampa was not paved, and he described it as a huge dust storm. Near Fallujah they found an IED.

On arrival at Camp Al Qaim, the battalion (3/7) realized that the MP platoon had Humvees with heavy machine guns on them, so they put the MPs as a provisional rifle company with Weapons Company. At first, they did mounted patrols. Lance Corporal Allen said that the MPs joke that MP does not really mean "Military Police", it means "Multi-Purpose" because there are so many different things they can do. He said that it wasn't until they established the Iraq Police Academy that the MPs began to do more traditional roles.

He said that the way that MPs were assigned to work the new academy was partly based on which Marines were more comfortable with the weapons systems that would be used on the patrols in the towns.

In late March and early April the Marine infantry did most of the patrolling in Husaybah. The first class of IPs was still being trained when the fighting broke out in mid-April. The first police graduating class went to the city of Karabilah. The current class will be going to Husaybah.

When the fighting began on April 17, the MPs were part of a convoy that took part of the 3/7 battalion staff to join the battalion commander (Lieutenant Colonel Lopez) in Husaybah. Once in the city, "They actually punched us out down Market Street [towards Lima Company's position]." He said that he didn't know why things happened the way they did; some of them call it the "Luck of the MPs." He gave an example of seeing RPG positions, turning around to take out the shooters, and then an IED would go off where they had been just minutes before.

"The whole time it felt like boot camp, down in the pits, pullin' down targets, and the rounds crackin' and poppin' overhead."

Allen estimated that they were awake for at least 24 hours. When they finally got a short break of about four hours, many of the Marines were able to grab some rest. During this break, he saw a Cobra helo fire several missiles into a building in Husaybah. "I never seen anything like that before."

MPs were then sent to Force Recon's position in the western part of the city along Trash Road, bringing their Humvee-mounted M240 Golf machine guns, Mark 19s (grenade launcher), or the M2 .50 caliber machine guns. He said that while trying to eat some chow, they had to drop everything when shooting started and then move to their defensive positions. Once the "all clear" was passed, they went back and continued eating.

The MPs were then used to form a cordon around a building for a Force Recon raid that produced several detainees. That night, they went to the Syria-Iraq border to ensure that no fighters snuck across the border to join the violence.

When the fighting was over, the platoon was split into two parts: One for operations in and around the area, and the other for running the IP training academy. On a typical day for Allen's part of the platoon, Operations, many Marines find time to start with PT early while it's still cool. Their lieutenant will come and tell them what time they'll be moving out. Often they will go out in to Karabilah or Husaybah, go to a police station and set up a defensive position, while some of the Marines there will go out on patrol with the IPs. This is usually a five-hour operation, but if something happens while they are in town, they get called to assist, whether to cordon off an area with an IED, or to escort the battalion commander. The battalion likes having the MPs in town; it gives them another element there.

Allen said that, "Two days ago, we rolled out of town, 10 minutes after we left that intersection [Train and East End], there's an RPG attack on Weapons Company." Once again, the luck of MPs came into play. I remarked that maybe when they demobilize this time they should all go to Las Vegas. Lance Corporal Allen replied, "We did that the last time!"

Lance Corporal Daniel Patrick Baute
Military Policeman, 2nd Platoon, Charlie MP Company, attached to 3/7

This Marine Reservist found out about his second deployment to Iraq at the unit's November 2003 Marine Corps Birthday celebration. He was active in training the local police force: "You can definitely tell the difference between the trained Iraqi police and the police that have not been trained yet."

Baute joined the Marine Corps Reserve while a freshman in college, went to MCRD San Diego, and has now been in the Corps for two years. After his initial training, Baute was out of active-duty training for three weeks, went to one reserve drill weekend, and then learned that the unit was being mobilized to go to Iraq! During the first deployment, the unit was attached to FSSG, and later to the Army's 716th MP Battalion. "We mostly did convoy operations in southern Iraq and northern Kuwait, with some EPW [enemy prisoner of war] handling, and force protection."

The MP Company got back to its home base in October 2003, and at the November Marine Corps Ball, learned that it would remain on active duty and return to Iraq for OIF II. "After the ceremony and activities, Staff Sergeant King and our platoon commander called us to one of the hotel rooms and pretty much told us that we would be reactivated for OIF II." He said that the Marines were all pretty much "blind-sided" by this news, since none of them expected this announcement.

In November they went to do MOUT training in Alabama, and then to 29 Palms, California for SASO training. Training completed, they flew to Kuwait in mid-February, and then convoyed up into Husaybah in western Iraq. En route, the convoy made stops at several Army camps in Iraq. He said that they were told in Kuwait that they would be attached to 3/7, and that their main mission would be working with the Iraqi police.

On arrival at Camp Al Qaim, the infantry units did ride-alongs with their Army counterparts, but the MPs did not go on these rides. During the first week at Camp Al Qaim, the MPs began formulating the plans for the police academy here, and working on force protection issues for the academy.

Lance Corporal Baute said, "I'm involved with the operations going out in town. So far, we've gone to two police stations. The Karabilah police station was the first one, and we stayed there for about four days, set up force protection, and we were, Kilo was actually a couple buildings behind us, and they were our QRF. And Engineers helped build our force protection there. And then, about two weeks ago, we were in Husaybah, the police station there, and we again stayed about four nights there. And this time it was a Kilo platoon that was attached to Lima out in Husaybah. They helped our operations and also the Engineers, build force protection out in Husaybah."

He was not out in town while the fighting happened in Husaybah in mid-April. "We were at the police academy when things started goin' on in Husaybah, and we were brought back to base. When we got back here, we were put on QRF for, I believe, Kilo." The second half of the MP platoon went out into Husaybah, to serve with the QRF for Lima Company there.

The police academy was located about two miles from Camp Al Qaim, at a phosphate plant. At the academy, about half of the MPs there were providing protection for the camp, while the rest conducted the training as instructors. Each operating day there was about 10 to 12 hours long. Currently Baute is not involved in this training, but he said that every couple of weeks the Marines in town switch out with those at the academy.

I asked about his work in the towns. "You can definitely tell the difference between the trained Iraqi police and the police that have not been trained yet." The trained police have a gold pin that they wear, showing that the Marines have trained them. "They definitely wear the pin with pride." Lance Corporal Baute said that these policemen carry themselves with pride, and try to help the less-experienced police. Still, he said that Marines still have to be careful when working with the police, as not all may be reliable.

The Iraqi police get training with the AK 47 and the Glock pistol. They test fire these weapons, get weapons safety instruction, and learn how to break down the weapons for cleaning and maintenance.

Currently, his part of the platoon goes out to the police stations in Karabilah and Husaybah. There were more visits to Husaybah, especially during a three-day strike by the police there. An Iraqi police colonel had led some sort of petition drive that led to the strike—he has since been relieved of duty. From a 30-man Marine MP platoon, about 15 go into town at a time. In Husaybah, they often go out on patrols with the IPs.

They have also gone out with some of the Marine infantry squad patrols. "It's a little bit more high-paced when we're out there," he said. But even when not out in town for a four-day stretch, they still go out in town for a four-hour period to check on the Iraqi patrols, insuring that they are wearing their protective gear (helmets, flak jackets), carrying their weapons properly, manning their posts and going out on patrols. "It's tough to get [some of] them to do their job. Some of them, it's just a paycheck."

The IPs work 12 hours, then are off for 24 hours before their next shift. Lance Corporal Baute feels that some of the IPs really want to work to make their city better.

Now that his platoon is halfway through the deployment, most of the Marines want to get back on regular reserve status. They hope that the job in Iraq will get done. Baute wants to get back and continue college. If he had not been called to active duty, he would be graduating from college in another year. But he ended by noting, "It's what we signed up for."

Corporal Ryan David Griffey
Weapons Instructor and Gunner, Truck Platoon, MHG, attached to 3/7

This Motor Transport Marine helped move Kilo Company Marines into Husaybah on April 17: "Myself, I was a 240 gunner that day ... It was probably the closest combat I've been in. Any combat before, with OIF I, this was the closest I've engaged the enemy. They were anywhere from 50 to 1,000 meters."

Corporal Griffey has been with MHG for the past three years, and served in Iraq in 2003. Previously he served at Guantanamo, Cuba.

His primary MOS is as a truck driver, but to help his platoon he instructs these Marines in the crew-served weapons (.50 cal machine gun, 240 Golf, SAW), personal weapons, and weapons techniques. About once a month the Marines fire on weapons ranges to keep proficient. He explained that the Motor T Marines have to learn different firing techniques than the infantrymen: "Our guys are actually firing from either a moving vehicle or on top of a 7-ton [Tactical Truck with 7-ton capacity], so it's a little more difficult to have to fire along with their target moving." Also, the drivers train to spot IEDs while they drive.

Griffey learned that he would be returning to Iraq when he came back from leave, about two weeks before the trip here. During this short time, he worked to help BZO (battle sight) the weapons of his Marines. When his Motor T unit arrived in Iraq, they fell in on vehicles left to 3/7 by units from OIF I. These vehicles were in decent shape, and the Motor T Marines worked on them for about a week. "Now, all our vehicles are pretty much all up." They work with about 30 vehicles, all but one from OIF I. Four vehicles came off MPF shipping.

Corporal Griffey explained that his whole Motor T Platoon was not with 3/7: "We have some Marines from Wing units from Cherry Point [NC], we have Marines from TSB out of Camp LeJeune [NC], also have Marines from Medical Battalion. We have detachments to MHG." He said that many of these drivers were newly licensed, some for Humvees, some for the trucks.

When 3/7 left Kuwait, they drove into Iraq, north of Nasariyah, stayed overnight, then drove out early the next morning, starting at about 0400. There was almost no resistance for the first two days. On the second night they stopped at an Army camp, and arrived at Camp Al Qaim on the third night. 3/7 moved up into Iraq in three "sticks", and Griffey was with the third stick. The second stick encountered small arms fire one day during the move. During the third day, a partly completed IED was discovered and disarmed. Al Qaim had been mortared that day, so when 3/7 arrived at the camp, they had to move the Marines to their quarters quickly. The camp's motor pool had been hit by mortar fire, but no Marines were injured. This motor pool was moved to another area of the camp.

"There was supposed to be a 30-day turnover [with the Army], but it ended up lasting only two weeks." The area is easy to navigate around, with well-developed main roads, so the Marines learned the area quickly. The Left-seat, Right-seat rides went without incident during these two weeks. The mortar attacks continued, and the IEDs picked up in number.

The main mission of the truck drivers was to deliver Marines where needed quickly, but the gunners on the gun trucks (Humvees) also provide heavy gunfire support with their crew-served weapons when needed. It takes less than 30 seconds to dismount an infantry squad from one of the vehicles.

"Within a month we started running convoys full-time from Husaybah, resupplying the Firm Base we had there, resupplying them with water, MREs, chow, mail. And also running down to Al Assad to pick up the resupplies for Al Qaim."

Now there was a helo supply line, and the helos airdrop in water, MREs, UGRs (Unit Group Rations), and parts for vehicles. The trucks move these supplies from the flight line (where I arrived at the camp) up to 3/7's supply area.

Currently, some of the Motor T Marines are attached out to Lima Company in Husaybah as part of the QRF there. Others are part of the QRF for Camp Al Qaim, attached to India Company.

On April 17 when the big fighting began in Husaybah, the Motor T Marines got called up to respond to the attacks on Lima Company.

"By 1500 we had loaded up all of Kilo Company, and everybody in our platoon except the three that were at Lima, were out there escorting with our gun trucks. We then proceeded down the east side of the city of Husaybah, where as soon as we stopped the vehicles, we let the infantry dismount, we started receiving sniper fire, and some RPG fire."

As the Kilo Marines started their sweep through the city, the Motor T Marines' mission was to secure the east end of the road where they were. The mission there lasted about 72 hours.

"Myself, I was a 240 gunner that day. It was mounted on one of our TVRs [MTVR—Medium Tactical Replacement Vehicle, a 7-ton heavy duty tactical all-terrain vehicle]. It was probably the closest combat I've been in. Any combat before, with OIF I, this was the closest I've engaged the enemy. They were anywhere from 50 to 1,000 meters. A lot of our Marines, it was their first time in combat, their reaction time tended to be a little slower than myself and other experienced Marines, which is understandable. They started to respond probably within the first five minutes."

Some of the vehicles were in bad positions, near tall buildings and unfinished IEDs. After the first 12 hours, the firing slowed down somewhat, but the truckers only engaged in two firefights with small groups of individuals. A mortar hit near their position, but the shooters carrying the mortar tube were spotted about 1,000 meters southeast of their position. Corporal Griffey engaged them with his 240 Golf. The shooters ran into a small shack (about 15 × 20 feet). "We called in, as they were pretty much out of our range, hiding in the building, we called in one of the CAAT teams." This team moved towards the building and finally engaged this enemy with explosives. After the shack was hit, the Marines found remains of RPGs and mortars. It had been a small weapons cache.

Things were quiet that night (April 17) and 3/7 planned a sweep of the city from north to south, trying to push any enemy fighters towards the truckers' position. By the third day, two infantry platoons loaded up onto the vehicles and moved to the southwest part of the city. They then went to Lima's Firm Base. There was sporadic mortar and small arms fire on the base. Drivers who had NVGs for night driving ran into problems when their batteries began to wear down, and helo support was limited during the fighting.

Things have been relatively quiet since then. The trucks now have armored doors and ballistic glass (three to four inches thick) for the windshields.

Kilo Company has been doing humanitarian missions requiring transportation about twice a month in the area, and this also provides good reconnaissance of routes and land features of the area. During one of these missions, infantry would sweep through a town. The tempo was slower, but IEDs remained a concern.

Last year Corporal Griffey was in Nasariyah and Al Kut. He said it was a "little bit more up-front fighting." More of what you'd think of as a war—platoons of enemy, mortar rounds landing on targets. An Iraqi tank division and two infantry companies near Nasariyah attacked his unit.

This year it is more terrorist, guerrilla hit-and-run fighting by the enemy fighters. Lots of fire and run, setting up IEDs. He said that ambushes are more popular with the enemy this year.

As for the civilians, he said that there were protests last year in Nasariyah, but this year the people in Husaybah seem to be more friendly.

Corporal Christopher Logan Cahill
Motor T Operator, Truck Platoon, 1 MHG

Corporal Cahill volunteered to deploy to Iraq with 3/7. Initially he drove vehicles to support the build-up of camps for Kilo and Lima Companies, later helping to bring Kilo Marines to the fight in Husaybah.

Corporal Cahill entered recruit training in 2000, and graduated that August. His first deployment was to 7th Comm, in Okinawa, Japan, for two years. He served three months in Thailand, and three months in Australia, and volunteered to serve in OIF I, but was not called to go. He was serving with the 2nd Marine Air Wing at Cherry Point, NC, when another call for volunteers came, this time from 3/7. He volunteered to go and here he is!

"I was only with the Air Wing for about a month when they got the call, and immediately, it was right then and there. I checked in and checked out and got sent over to 2nd MSG." He did some tests with the new 7-ton truck and was sent to the Middle East.

He said that the deployment wasn't exactly what he expected. He and another Marine came over on a new Air Force C5 transport jet with a load of weapons and parts. They spent two nights in Spain before they hit Kuwait. "Once we got to Kuwait, we stood our guard at the air strip in Kuwait, met up with our platoon, distributed all the gear, got everything up and running as soon as we got to Kuwait."

They then had a three-day, three-night drive to move up to Al Qaim. He said it was a tough drive, and felt over-prepared for the possible resistance through Iraq. He said that he felt settled in once he arrived at Camp Al Qaim. "Most of our operations on the way up here and around here are done at night." It makes it harder for the enemy to accomplish their goals at night. All drivers, A-drivers and gunners, have NVGs.

The Army was closing up operations, and had taken their job seriously. The Army bases had helped on the convoy up into Iraq, too.

Once the Army left, much of his work was in convoys, taking Marines to set up Firm Bases for Kilo and Lima Companies. The Lima Firm Base is right on the border with Syria, and it took a convoy about every other night for two weeks to get those Marines settled there. He said that the local enemy observed and saw the tempo of Marine operations. There were fewer Marines here than the Army had had. Corporal Cahill said that the enemy noticed, but that, "This was their first mistake."

Cahill said that attacks started to pick up in that first month here (March 2004). "They [the insurgents] started studying how we would respond in convoy movements, small arms fire, IEDs, bombs, explosions, booby trap-wise that they can possibly set up, even dummies to see how we would react."

He said that as the enemy adapted, the attacks started to get worse and worse. On the return trip from a supply convoy to the Lima Firm Base in Husaybah, a few mortar rounds were laid in the street and the Marines bypassed them. This was on Route Bronze in Husaybah.

In mid-April, Truck Platoon brought all of Kilo Company to Husaybah for the two sweeps into the city. Once the Kilo Marines were dropped off and began the attack, the trucks were left outside the city to wait for the return of the rifle company. They expected the mission to last 24 hours, but it lasted 72. He has spoken with many of the Marines who were in the city.

On April 18, Truck Platoon got into some sporadic firefights on the outskirts of the city. Some mortar fire hit about 300 meters south of their position. Eventually gun trucks from the CAAT platoon got involved in suppressing the mortar fire, and finding a weapons cache site. Later, Corporal Griffey was in the alleyway with other Marines, and was fired upon by insurgents. Cahill and Marines with him covered Griffey with small arms fire.

On April 19, a handful of Iraqis brought in a boy who had been shot through (the exit wound was near his kidney). A Navy Corpsman began to treat the boy. When Marines from Kilo found out about the wounded boy, they said that the boy had apparently been a signalman for the other terrorists and insurgents, using pigeons to signal Marine movements. Kilo Marines said that they had earlier shot at this signalman with a 240 Golf. The boy was evacuated by helicopter.

Cahill said, "We did notice that the people bringing out wounded were detainees that we had had before." Some of these Iraqis still had their number markings on them from when they had been held in cells. The Marines then realized that the wounded boy had been part of a group that had a weapons cache nearby.

Later on the 19th, during a resupply of ammo and chow, a 7-ton truck took a round through the windshield that bounced around inside the cab and wounded a Marine in the leg. Another truck was hit by an RPG that did not detonate, but it blew a hole in a fuel tank. "No casualties on Truck Platoon side." That night they returned to the camp.

It has been mostly quiet after mid-April. "Since then, I think we've had maybe four serious IED attacks. They're pretty much scared." The locals are more cooperative. There have not been any small arms attacks on any of their convoys, and they have been "lucky" in catching IEDs before they can be detonated.

He said, "I'm glad to be a part of it, but I do fear that ... once we leave here, it's going back to square one. I don't want to leave these people alone, or even let these people try to run themselves just yet, [because] there's just too many out there that are against this whole thought that these people need to be free." He said that the people need our help and he wouldn't have a problem staying here to help them. Mature words from this young Marine.

★ ★ ★

That ended a day of about 14 interviews that I was able to get to, and there were more Marines that Major Piedmont and I could not see today. I went to bed exhausted at 2200. It was tough to get situational awareness with this high volume of material, but it was such an opportunity to talk to these Marines, we both persevered. Normally, I could use late afternoons or early evenings to do summaries, but today they'd have to wait. I did "dump" the recordings onto the computer to make room in the memory of the Olympus voice recorder, and cleared out the digital camera so I had room for new photos of all subjects. When I had first gotten to 3/7, I had been given a briefing at a map of Husaybah, so some of what today's Marines told me made some sense. The next day, I would ride into Husaybah and actually see many of the areas that had been described to me today.

CHAPTER 3

Marines of Lima Company

Wednesday June 2, 2004: Camp Husaybah

A big day lined up for Major John Piedmont and me. First on our schedule was a convoy to the Marine camp in Husaybah. The convoy comprised seven vehicles, including gun trucks and up-armored Hummers, with all personnel riding in them armed. We had to meet outside the battalion COC beforehand for a convoy brief—what to do if an IED went off, actions to take in an ambush, call signs and radio frequencies. Everyone except me had at least an M16 A4; I had my 9mm pistol, which is only good for REALLY close targets.

I was very nervous throughout the whole 35-minute ride, as IEDs were still a threat, and there were piles of dirt and trash all over as we approached the town of Karabilah, just outside of Husaybah. I sat in the back seat of the Humvee, and Lieutenant Colonel Lopez showed me how he traced the movement of his vehicles on his "Blue Tracker" computer screen, and pointed out areas where some of the heavy fighting had taken place in April. He showed me the area where his Humvee had been hit by an RPG ambush, wounding him. We then turned left and drove south along the eastern part of Husaybah, then to the railroad tracks on the southern part of the town, then north to the police station. Lieutenant Colonel Lopez continued to narrate the events that have taken place in this city.

Lopez had us driven to a local police station just outside of Lima Company's camp. In the lot outside of this station, the Humvees spread out into a 360-degree security formation. Every Marine was armed and alert to anything that might happen. Lieutenant Colonel Lopez invited me to go inside the station with him as he met with two Iraqis. One guy was in his thwab, a traditional full-length cotton robe, and obviously had just gotten up, the other was in civilian clothes, and spoke some English. Lopez wanted info about a recent IED attack which had injured five Iraqi policemen, and offered a reward of $5,000 to find out who had carried it out. It was interesting to see the dynamics of this in action—little bits of information given to him and things hinted at. The Iraqis then brought in a handful of large (about one foot long) metal shards that they said were from that IED blast. The colonel asked to take some pieces (for later analysis by EOD).

Then we got back into the convoy vehicles and went on to the Lima Company's Firm Base camp. It is adjacent to the town of Husaybah itself, and right on the border with Syria: the HESCO Barriers are on the edge of the neutral zone, and Syria lies about 50 meters away. On the camp was a tower about 45 feet high, and Major Piedmont and I climbed the spiral staircase to get to the observation post (OP) on the top. From this height, we could see eastward across the entire city of Husaybah. Almost directly below us and to our north were buildings used to inspect items entering Iraq, and to our west was a small Syrian village that serves as the border crossing into that country. We cautiously took some photos from this vantage point.

Lance Corporal Daniel Rene Johnston
Team Leader, 2nd Squad, 1st Platoon, Lima Company, 3/7

I conducted this interview in a large cement-walled building with a metal roof. The windows were blacked out with old MRE cases to keep light from leaking out at night. Major Piedmont set up on the other side of this large room for his interviews. I sat on a cot to do my interviews here.

Lance Corporal Johnston enlisted in August 2001, just out of high school.

"I was pretty motivated comin' in the Marine Corps, something new that I was looking forward to do." He modestly stated that he graduated meritoriously as a Private First Class (a genuine honor for

Marine recruits). After SOI, he joined 3/7 at 29 Palms, and has been with 1st Platoon in Lima Company ever since.

He received extensive training on ranges, went to Mountain Warfare Training at Bridgeport, urban warfare training, and combined arms exercises.

He was with 3/7 in 2003, and trained for several months prior to going into Iraq as part of OIF I. He said, "It was pretty exciting." However, he did not enjoy wearing the MOPP suit and the gas mask while riding in AAVs: "It wasn't too fun at all."

In Baghdad he got into a couple of engagements where he dismounted, one of which he called "the battle of the Clover Leaf." It was a small arms fight. A car came and tried to run him down, but he shot at the car with his SAW. He went to a couple of Saddam's palaces, but did not find anything. "There was always nobody there when we got there." I remarked, "The Iraqis beat you to it!" and he laughed. Then he spent the next four months in Karbala before returning to the States. "We pulled humanitarian ops and we were just trying to help the people, so we ended up just stayin' in there."

He continued, "After a while I got the name for myself as a 'bullet magnet,' 'cause every time we went out, I seemed to get engaged. And it was just me. I'm either really, really unlucky or really lucky."

Lima Company left Iraq in September 2003. "Couple months later we found out we were coming back again." They trained, went back to the ranges, got some new Marines, tried to teach them as much as they could. He was a squad leader at that time. "I tried to train my guys to the best of my ability, and then we came here."

After arrival at Camp Al Qaim in late March 2004, Lima Company moved to Husaybah in Army Bradley fighting vehicles. Johnston said that the current Firm Base was very unsecured then; anyone could walk in from any angle. There were no barriers for protection. "It's amazing what we've done to the place." He continued, "From there, we started kickin' off the patrols with the Bradleys. It wasn't too big of a deal, they'd drive us around and we'd look at stuff."

He said that it was still hard to get oriented then. He explained that the Army was still here, and had the large Bradley fighting vehicles available to drive the Marines around the area. The Army also had their Abrams tanks with them. Once the Army left, all that his company had was a couple of Humvees. "For the first couple weeks, the only people gettin' hit were the Humvees." Lance Corporal Johnston said that they were hitting the "double-stack anti-tank mines."

He said that after the local enemy saw that the Marines were sending out more foot-mobile patrols, they started changing their tactics. He said insurgents were putting out little 60mm mortar shells set up as IEDs, 155mm shells, and some were wire-detonated while others were wireless.

"They'd pretty much place 'em on corners, and hit us wherever."

He said that the enemy would get a good distance from the IED and have visibility, so that they could more easily escape once they detonated the explosive charge. Johnston said that lately it has been very quiet compared to those early weeks in Husaybah.

He described an action from April 8. "We had set up a patrol base that night, and we were supposed to stay there for like, 72 hours. And the next morning, I was just getting back from a patrol, took off my boots, you know, try to get a couple hours' sleep. Not five minutes after that we started takin' direct fire from a house from down the alleyway, and from buildings across the street. I slapped on my boots and my gear as quick as I could. Rounds were flyin' through the house at such a high rate. They were everywhere. Actually, I pretty much had to low-crawl to the stairs to get to the top of the roof where I found the rest of the squad that was out on top. The reason they attacked us is they were ambushing a squad that had just left the Firm Base."

That squad was targeted with an RPG that missed, and was followed with small arms fire.

"When I got top of the roof, I could visualize, I could see everything now. I could see insurgents firing from rooftops in the corner, they had us pretty pinned down in the corner. And they saw us on the roof, started layin' fire to the roof. At that time I had to spread people out 'cause they were all clustered. Everybody wanted to get a piece of the action, I don't blame 'em."

Then one of 1st Squad's Marines got hit in the arm. Lance Corporal Johnston took him back and fixed up his arm. He then took a fire team, headed downstairs, and went to go flank where the insurgents were shooting.

"Got up there, a lot of fire was still comin' out. At that time CAAT, I think they were already on the way with their Humvees and .50 cals. And they got there, and we were still shootin', we could still see people on rooftops, still shooting at them. The other squad that was on the ground first, they moved up, none of them got hit, thankfully. They moved up and proceeded to push the insurgents back, east, towards the higher ground. As we flanked from the side, we ended up gettin' on one of the roofs, and firing from there. 'Course we had to get down, .50 cal started shootin' at us, they didn't know that we were up there. So that wasn't a good deal. So, we ended up gettin' down. We had 'em held up in a house, somehow they managed to escape, but either way, we had 'em held up in a house."

Once the Marines entered the house, they found a few AKs that were still hot, some RPGs and grenades. The Marines swept the area looking for these insurgents, and in buildings in the area found more RPGs and AKs that were loaded up and ready to shoot. Johnston felt that the insurgents were planning a running fight against the Marines into the town.

"All they had to do was bound back to a house, shoot at us, go back to another house, continue on."

The initial fight had stopped this insurgent plan cold. But the Marines did not capture or kill any of these insurgents that day.

Johnston said that they then returned to their little patrol base, planning to stay there until the next morning. He left the squad there as security, and went out on patrol with another squad. This patrol went west across the street towards a graveyard where a lot of IEDs had been found. A Marine had been hit there before. He said it was a real bad area. His patrol saw another Marine patrol walking through the graveyard. Lance Corporal Johnston then saw a very large explosion, about the sound of a 155 round exploding. "From there, I saw a Kevlar (helmet) fly about 30 feet in the air, and I was like, oh my God, this is not good. And, it wasn't even two minutes prior to that, that an IED, a different patrol from 1st Platoon got hit."

Johnston gathered up a Corpsman and a couple of other Marines to go help.

"We got over there, saw about four bodies were hurt, two of 'em pretty bad. One of 'em was my good friend Wasser, who I went to immediately with Doc, 'cause he was the worst. And, he had taken multiple shrapnel wounds to the upper torso, his lower limbs, his fingers were all gone. His face was beat up pretty bad. He had shrapnel in his neck. At that time, I took my trauma shears; proceeded to cut off all his clothes, gear, take everything off of him. We started doin' work. Couple of the guys I just went to, assessed really quickly, while the rest of the original platoon was comin' down to help. There was one guy, wasn't as bad off, but still missing a couple fingers, legs—kinda mangled."

There was one Marine who had been folded in half from the force of the IED blast. Johnston and the Navy Corpsmen worked on him until the medevac came. This Marine died while on the medevac chopper. The Marines could not find the triggerman for this IED.

Lance Corporal Johnston and his patrol then continued on their patrol, south into the city. They noticed a vehicle, a white car that was shadowing their movements, so they called up CAAT that was still in the area. CAAT then went to the car, stopped and searched it, and interrogated the driver.

Shortly after this, a firefight broke out in the area between the foot patrol and the Humvees. The squad that Johnston was with engaged insurgents who were bounding from building to building. They then returned to the Firm Base.

Johnston said that the memorial service for Wasser was tough for him, as he had known him his whole time in the Fleet.

On April 17, about 22 mortar rounds hit the Lima Firm Base in Husaybah. Marines went out to do crater analysis to determine the origin direction of the mortars. They could hear the sound of fighting in the town of Husaybah. There was one unexploded mortar round, and as Johnston went to take pictures of it, two more mortar rounds landed about 70 meters away.

"Scared the crap outta me, I tell you what! Out there all by myself. So those hit, I left. As I was leavin' I saw the React with Weapons Platoon goin' out. I gave 'em a good luck wave as they were leavin'."

Then the Marines at the Firm Base started to double up on the posts. He later learned that Weapons had gone way, way east. And also that the Company Commander had died that day, along with five Marines, all guys that he had known. All day, Marines on the high posts at the Firm Base were taking shots at insurgents.

"I was up on some of the posts, and I could see them comin' out with children in front of them, you know, real guerrilla-type tactics."

1st Platoon stayed on the base to secure it. Johnston said that some newspapers called the Base the Alamo, but he felt that it was not an Alamo, as the Marines were out in the town attacking the enemy, and the Base was not overrun.

"I don't think that there wasn't a post, except the one facing Syria, that didn't get a chance to shoot somebody. Two of my guys from my squad, ended up killing a couple people [insurgents]. I remember walking up to the post when one of the guys was pretty shooken up about it. You know, you kill somebody you tend to get a little nervous."

As the fighting continued, an insurgent anti-tank round was fired at their post. "One round zoomed by us, hit the wood, thankfully, in front of me and [I] got splintered in the face. I'd rather get splinters in the face than the round." As night fell, the firing slowed down. From an ICDC compound next to the base, someone started to fire at the base, and Johnston had his SAW gunner open up on the compound.

The next day began a battalion-wide sweep of the city. They searched every house from north to south about a click into the city. As they began the search, they could see the aftermath of the prior fighting in the city. The Baath Party headquarters building was in ruins. A team from 3rd Squad set up an OP in the ruins, and a couple of minutes later an IED went off in the building. No one was hurt, fortunately.

"From there we started searching the houses one by one." There was no contact that day. Lance Corporal Johnston wound up standing on top of a bag with a 155 round. Someone noticed a wire sticking out from the bag. People started running away from him, and finally he ran away from the round. He said it was good that no one (of the insurgents) was observing this, as there were about eight Marines standing around at that time. During that day the Marines found a lot of AKs and IEDs.

For a couple of weeks after that, all enemy activity stopped. No small arms fire, no IED attacks. "Apparently, the word was we had put a big dent in the mujahideen's, pretty much their corps. We had destroyed about a hundred or so of what they were sayin' of the mujahideen."

He said that the people in Husaybah were overall pleased, as most of the dead were insurgents. The Marines then went back to everyday patrols, and slowly the IED attacks have picked up again. A few days ago a Marine was slightly wounded by an IED explosion during a patrol.

I asked if any Iraqis are involved in the patrols. He said that the ICDC has always been there with the patrols, but a few days ago the local police quit en masse. The local police have recently re-occupied the police station. He feels that the ICDC are more military and trustworthy.

"There's always a danger every day we go out there." He stresses this with his Marines.

I then asked him to compare OIF I and current operations. Last year they could see the enemy and know what they were looking for. It was easier to engage the enemy then. This year the IED threat is constant, and it's tough to find an enemy who is waiting to push a button.

Lance Corporal Johnston said that he has met a lot of good local people out in town on posts. He has had tea with some of them.

Corporal Jason Alan Lemcke
Squad Leader, 3rd Squad, 1st Platoon, Kilo Company, attached to Lima Company, 3/7

After weeks of patrols and finding IEDs, the squad's first firefight took place on April 8 near the "Crack House." During the fighting on April 17, the squad helped to guard the south gate of Camp Husaybah, and participated in the sweep of the town on April 18.

Corporal Lemcke had just returned from a patrol this morning, and I asked him to give a little of his Marine Corps background before reviewing events in Iraq.

"January 2001 is when I came into the Marine Corps. Went through Boot Camp at San Diego." After SOI, he went to Security Forces School in June 2001, and then reported to 2nd FAST Company in Yorktown, VA where he served until July 2003.

He did one overseas deployment, where he trained with British Royal Marines, and has been involved in many refuelings of nuclear submarines. During March and April of OIF I, his platoon deployed with Seal Team 4 to conduct interdiction operations just off the coast of Syria. Then in May 2003, he returned to Rota Spain. He participated in "STROG" (Strait of Gibraltar) missions out of Gibraltar, where, "Basically we board ships coming through the Straits of Gibraltar, to prevent terrorists from attacking the ships. Trying to prevent a USS *Cole* incident."

In July 2003, 15 of these FAST Marines were picked to provide security for relief forces in Monrovia, Liberia. Also they would be a sort of advance party should larger Marine forces be sent there. The civil war broke out again while they were there, and they participated in providing enhanced security for the U.S. Embassy in Monrovia. They returned to Rota Spain in August 2003, and to Yorktown in September.

Corporal Lemcke reported to Kilo Company in November 2003. "Then in February 2004, I found myself in Husaybah, Iraq." He was initially assigned as a fire team leader to refresh his infantry skills, and soon was appointed squad leader.

From Camp Udari, Kuwait in March 2004, they prepared to go into Iraq. He outlined the ground convoy movement up into Iraq, with several stops including Camp Al Assad and Camp Al Qaim (then known as FOB Tiger). Six hours after arriving at Al Qaim, they moved to the Lima Company Firm Base in Husaybah. The Army drove Marine leaders around the area in Bradley fighting vehicles. Lemcke said, "They did a good job of turnover. They showed us some points, all kind of bad areas around the town, overall they handed us a good picture of the threat in the AO."

The Marines took over on March 12, 2004. He said, "I remember for the first four or five days, there was no contact at all. It was actually pretty quiet, 'cause we saturated the city with foot patrols. We knew that the Army really hasn't been a big influence on foot patrols through the whole city, mainly relying on the Bradley fighting vehicles."

CAAT Red took its first casualties after this, and it seemed that CAAT Red was taking casualties from IEDs every day after that. Also, he couldn't remember the date, but two Marines in the CAAT section hit a double-stacked landmine southeast of the city that blew the Humvee they were in "practically in half."

CAAT Red was replaced by CAAT Blue because of the number of casualties CAAT Red had been receiving.

Corporal Lemcke said casualties were happening every day or every few days. On April 1 his platoon got pulled back to Camp Al Qaim for a proposed regimental operation. Between then and April 6, they trained extensively to do cordons and detentions of suspected insurgents. He remembered that the regiment caught about 13 of the 20 individuals it was seeking.

Then his platoon went back to Camp Husaybah on April 8. Three hours later, they were out on patrol on the streets of the town. The Marines were expecting some sort of retaliation after their recent successful raid. There were many IEDs going off. He said that one was the biggest explosion that he ever heard, and it was several blocks away from him. He said that the three Marines who were on top of it miraculously survived because the 155mm round had been buried too deep by the insurgents. They did not find the insurgents who were setting these off.

Later that night he went out on a patrol at about 2200. "I remember we were patrolling north of the city, and one of my team leaders heard a mortar come from way north of the city. Well, I decided to, could not really get a pinpoint, accurate pos [position], on the firing position. Heard it again. This time I heard it. Didn't hear any impact, so I was kinda skeptical about what it was. Then, I actually heard it about 150 meters just north of us. And it was no doubt in my mind where someone was firing. Then I diverted my squad from a patrol, went through all the vegetation north of the city, and didn't find anything. Did a few cordon and knocks."

Then he remembered that LAR (Light Armored Reconnaissance) was operating up north in a heavy gunfight, and set up a position to provide cover if needed. After about an hour he continued the patrol.

His team leaders asked him which route they would use to return to the Firm Base. Corporal Lemcke did not want to return via Trash Road because they had just used it. But he trusted the judgment of his team leaders, as they said that they were familiar with the route. At around 0100, an IED hit the tail end of his squad. "If it wasn't for the slope in the road, I woulda had at least two or three casualties." He could not find the detonator of this IED, and brought his squad back to the Firm Base.

By 1200 on April 9, his squad went out on patrol towards the south of the city. They moved towards the building they called the "Crack House," (Checkpoint 69) because of the many fights that took place near it. At around 1400 his squad was just north of Checkpoint 69 when the insurgents set up a direct-fire ambush that cut his squad in half with a heavy volume of fire.

"My first team leader, I told him to stay in place. 'I'll take my second team, the rest of the guys I have [to] make a movement on him'."

Corporal Lemcke's idea was to pressure the origin of the ambush. He then started to take fire from an individual with an AK on a building about 50 meters away. "I engaged, the shot wasn't really too good, I missed him." As they made movement, his second team was not where he had left them. This team leader had decided to push up on his own, after he had begun to take fire from another insurgent.

Lemcke thought that it was only a one- to two-man ambush, but in retrospect, felt that there were probably at least eight to ten insurgents. At one point, he saw a man standing behind a pole, and then noticed a facemask on the man when he poked his head out, holding an AK 47, marking him as an insurgent. "He was a good 75 meters from me. I then engaged him, my rounds hit the telephone pole, but deflected outward. Did not hit the individual." The individual started to run away.

As 1st Platoon was trying to get there to assist his squad, they took rifle and RPG fire. Lemcke's 1st Fire Team began to take fire, and went up to the top of the "Crack House" to set up an observation post. Lemcke linked up with some elements of 2nd Squad, an Army PSYOPS staff sergeant, and the Engineer platoon commander. They began movement on the enemy, and Lemcke coordinated with his own platoon commander, Lieutenant David Fleming. Corporal Lemcke then got the order to move to Checkpoint 69, west of where he was.

He said that a mujahideen fighter walked right out in front of him, but Lemcke had a faulty magazine and couldn't get off a shot at the man. The insurgent saw this, but did not shoot, and just ran away into a house. His Marines went into the house, but the man was gone.

He now tried to get communication with all elements of his squad. The different teams were all attempting to engage the enemy, and after about an hour linked up. The platoon linked up near Checkpoint 72, and Lemcke got contact with all of his squad again. They set up near the graveyard and did a few cordon and knocks to look for insurgents in the area. Lemcke said that all of his training allowed him to just do the things that he needed to do.

On April 17, he remembered waking up hearing that Lima 3 (3rd Platoon) was in heavy contact. Staff Sergeant Bankston, his platoon sergeant, had his Marines give up their frag grenades, 203 rounds, and AT4s to Lima 4 that was going out to support Lima 3. Lemcke knew that ammo would be resupplied later in the day when they went out. Staff Sergeant Bankston also said that there was a possibility that the ICDC might revolt against them, and that 300 mujahideen were in the city.

"We were ready to do something," said Lemcke. His squad was sent to the southern gate to defend against a possible vehicle-borne IED. They set up a Claymore mine, and set in his squad along a berm there. After two hours, Lieutenant Fleming gave them a Frag Order. There was a group near Checkpoint 80 south of the city. Lima 2 and Kilo 1 were going to coordinate an attack. They got more ammo, then moved around the 440 area of the city (he pointed this out on a wall map). When Kilo 1 got there, they moved around a six-foot high berm, with RPG rounds flying near them. His squad engaged and hit about two insurgents there in the 440 area of Husaybah. Lemcke also called in some close air support during the fighting. In one of the buildings they found hundreds of small arms rounds, empty magazines, and spent ammunition, all signs of very recent enemy fighting. They also found some pools of blood, but no bodies.

Soon after this the power in the city shut down, and things were quiet in his area. They moved back to the Firm Base and got ready for the sweep in the eastern part of Husaybah.

Lemcke's squad had a lane to search in the city, and searched every house in their area for about 13 to 14 hours. They found an AK 47 and a bandoleer of rounds, but little else in the houses.

At this point in the interview, our taping was interrupted by a loud BOOOM! I looked across at Major Piedmont on the other side of the room, then looked at Corporal Lemcke. Lemcke asked the other Marine that Major Piedmont was interviewing, "That a mortar?" The other Marine thought for a few seconds, then said, "Naw, I think they're test firing a 203."

It was a very loud noise, and sounded as if it was just outside the building that we were in. But these Marines at this camp have experienced mortar rounds landing on the camp and knew what they sounded like, so we had to trust their judgment. Both of these Marines sort of dismissed the noise, and our interviews resumed.

Back to Corporal Lemcke: On April 19, there was another small firefight. He heard some kind of launch come from the middle of the city, "And actually heard the projectile go over our heads, and land just north of 440. It wasn't an RPG. They said it was a Russian, 107mm like, missile. So, it was a pretty huge ordnance thrown at us." Corporal Lemcke said that for about the next three weeks there was almost no enemy activity in Husaybah. Recently there have been small attacks.

He said that about two weeks ago, the ICDC was giving lots of info about IEDs being placed near a mosque. His squad went down a road, and a short time afterwards, 2nd Squad, which followed the same route, found an IED in the middle of that road. Someone had placed the IED there between the two patrols. Before he brought his squad back, one of his Marines found a 155mm round in a bag near Trash Road. They set up a perimeter until EOD arrived to detonate the round. Shortly after this, they found two more IEDs hidden under piles of rocks along the side of the road.

Last night he was on a patrol on an OP looking towards Syria, looking for anyone trying to cross the border into Iraq.

Corporal Lemcke has done a few patrols with the ICDC, and has also done two patrols with Iraqi police. He said they still need more work to get ready for the turnover. "I led one actually with the Iraqi police."

When I asked if he had anything else to remember, he finished by saying, "It's all right there, sir, everything I've experienced."

Lieutenant Bradley Ryan Watson
3rd Platoon Commander, Lima Company, 3/7

When I met this young officer, I had no idea that he would give me one of the best combat interviews that I've had to date. He had a clear memory, and was collected in his thoughts. At times he needed to pause during the interview before he carefully told of the events he has experienced. He has obviously taken care to go over the events in his mind. He was at the building when Lima Company Commander Rich Cannon and others were found dead, and Watson informed the battalion commander of the loss.

The interview began with my routine questions about his background and training in the Corps. He graduated from Vanderbilt University in 2001, and worked as a television producer with CNN Washington before he joined the Marine Corps and received his commission in December 2002. After training at Quantico, he joined 3/7 on November 1, 2003, when Lieutenant Colonel Lopez told the battalion that it would be returning to Iraq. Much of the training concentrated on SASO.

"We arrived here in Husaybah the first week in March, and my platoon was tasked with the first city patrol, it was a joint patrol with the First of the Third ACR within the city." The patrol, that also had two Army Bradley fighting vehicles, was uneventful. The replacement in force (RIF) took place, and the first city patrol without the Army was also his 3rd Platoon, Lima Company.

"We were tasked with clearing and investigating the former Baath Party headquarters [at the] intersection of the east end of Market Street here in Husaybah. That very first patrol, we took our first enemy contact, which was an IED buried in the yard of the headquarters building. Resulted in zero casualties. It was an illum [illumination] canister filled with some kind of explosive, probably a Russian equivalent of C4."

Shortly after this they began to receive small arms fire. "We returned fire, cordoned off the house, the entire block, a platoon-size element. Went through and searched the house but didn't find the shooter." They continued the patrol and then returned to the Firm Base in Husaybah.

"In total, one in three Marines has a Purple Heart, some of them have two. On the 8th of April, my platoon was hit with three IEDs, one patrol, resulting in seven WIA and one KIA. It was Lance Corporal Christopher Walker. Actually standing on top of what was presumed to be a 60mm mortar round that was rigged to detonate."

Watson paused, then continued:

"I myself was wounded that day. The IEDs went off in sequence. There was one north of our route, one on our route, and one south of it. All three produced casualties. There was no small arms fire.

"I was medevacked, I was hit by the first IED. The second one hit north of us and the third one hit south of us, that was the one that caused two urgent surgicals and one KIA. It was the most serious ... I wasn't actually there for that one; I was medevacked after the first one, with shrapnel wounds to the lower extremities. And then heard over the radio as I was being driven back to BAS [Battalion Aid Station] here that my other squad had been hit with an IED, that was the last thing I heard over the radio as I handed over my map to my platoon sergeant so he could finish the route. And I came back and they cut off my trouser leg, and went to the COC and I could hear the rest of the contacts from here in the radio room. It's just very frustrating to hear that happening and you can't be out there."

Lieutenant Watson continued:

"We were medevacked after that to the Forward Operating Base Al Qaim, and then further medevacked to the hospital at Al Assad. I was treated there for a day and a half, then I was back into combat, out patrolling again on the 14th. I was back at Camp Husaybah on the 11th.

"On the 14th of April, I led my first combat patrol back into the city. We took up the patrol base, Checkpoint 69, which is commonly known as the 'Crack House'. I'd subdivided my zone into three sub-zones: One per squad. We were going to occupy that as a patrol base, Checkpoint 69. We took up a position on the roof; I briefed my order to my squad leaders. One squad leader was to remain, holding security there at the patrol base, and then the other two were going to go out on city patrols. Almost immediately after I wrapped the order up, two squad leaders departed the roof, my RO [radio operator] came up to the roof so I could radio in our sitrep. And then almost immediately as he keyed the mic, an IED that had been planted on the roof detonated, and nearly knocked all three of us off the roof. Checkpoint 69 is a three-story building, a tall three-story building, that used to be [an] apartment complex or a hotel. My RO had an eight-inch piece of wood stuck in his neck, my 2nd Squad leader had shrapnel in his foot, and I had no injuries. This IED was probably 25 feet from us. In fact, for all the six IEDs that have now been detonated on my platoon, we've had people within 25 feet of all of 'em. I've personally been within 25 feet of four of 'em."

"Now, the three of us are on the rooftop, I have two wounded, I myself am okay, and other Marines ran up to the roof to find out what happened. We took cover in the staircase. The Marine who took shrapnel in his foot could still walk, the Marine with wood in his neck was on the deck, hadn't realized he'd been injured yet. This all happened in the span of about three seconds."

Watson heard the RO call for help and he sent a Marine to help the RO back. Then, "About two minutes after the explosion, we started receiving small arms [fire], by that I mean former Soviet medium machine gun and AK 47 fire, from two separate enemy positions at about 90 degrees to our position: One almost due north of us, and one almost due east of us. Each position was no more than 100 to 150 meters from our patrol. We immediately returned fire, I remember distinctly hearing my SAW gunners open up from the second deck, suppress the enemy positions. And they [enemy] stopped firing.

"And then we exchanged fire intermittently for the next 45 minutes in what resulted in some 700-round firefight. We had 'eyes on' enemy to the east in white clothes with medium machine gun, takin' fire at us."

While this was happening a STA team attached to the platoon that had gone out to provide overwatch on an OP had just gotten to their position when they began to receive small arms fire. The seven Marines there had one urgent wound to the leg of one Marine, and Lieutenant Watson started to arrange for a medevac. Staff Sergeant T. Wilder, his former platoon sergeant, began to organize the medevac out of LZ Sparrow, which was just south of the patrol base location. Wilder took one squad with him to secure the LZ, and Watson stayed at the checkpoint to continue the gunfight.

"As it turned out, we were able to get the Blackhawk (U.S. Army UH-60 helo) in to evac the casualty that the STA team had taken. But, it started taking small arms fire almost immediately after it landed, had to take off again. So we re-routed the medevac back to Camp Husaybah, and they air-medevacked him from there, as well as my two casualties that occurred on the roof."

Lieutenant Watson backed up the story of the IED on the roof, saying that they had cleared the roof when they got up there. "There was a pile of wood and like scrap lumber. It had just been stacked on top of the roof. Inside of that pile of wood was some sort of explosive that was powerful enough to punch a hole in the six- to eight-inch concrete roof all the way through to the third level. And of course, blew all the wood off the pile. Part of that wood is what ended up in my radio operator's neck. He has since returned to duty. He's fine." The Marine with shrapnel in his foot has returned to the States.

"That day, April 8th, was the beginning of the rising action leading up to what has since been called the 'Easter Offensive', where insurgent and Iraqi forces here in Iraq increased the violence." He said that from the 8th through the 21st of April was the height of the conflict here, with the peak being around the 17th and 18th.

"There's a resolution between the 17th and the 21st. Between the 21st and the 1st of May, I don't think we took any contact in Husaybah at all."

"On the 14th it's important to say there were other things going on other than the firefight. A battalion convoy, including the battalion commander [Lieutenant Colonel Lopez], was ambushed on its way into the city. There are two choke points leading into the city, only two roads that can sustain our convoys into Husaybah from our Forward Operating Base Al Qaim. The opportunity for ambush is pretty good, from the enemy perspective. So at the same time we had the ambush goin' on, my firefight, the medevac, another Kilo 4 platoon was in a conflict of their own, three significant, simultaneous contacts within the city, which stretched out resources as far as medevac and React forces pretty thin."

Lieutenant Watson said it took the React force a while to get to him, and he eventually went on the offensive, but the enemy escaped because of the time that had elapsed.

He conducted a couple more platoon-size patrols from April 8 up to April 14 that were uneventful. Then, "On the 17th of April, we were scheduled to kick off a patrol at seven in the morning, through the city. About 0600, there was a patrol out, as you were, there was an OP out, with Force Recon. We started hearing about contacts in the city about 0730. One of the Force Recon OPs out there at the intersection of Market and East End, ambushed and killed four mujahideen just walking in broad daylight, occupied the Baath Party headquarters, and that sorta kicked off the entire battle.

"I'm sitting in the COC and I'm hearing reports from the watch officer that Lima 4, Lima Weapons, has been called out as QRF. CAAT Blue had been ambushed a couple times at the Baath Party headquarters and took heavy fire on their CAAT vehicles there that resulted in putting two TOW missiles into that building. And Lima 4 was heavily engaged on the east side of town. The casualties that occurred from those contacts needed to be medevacked, so I volunteered our platoon to secure LZ Nightingale, north of the city, north of Trash Road, to evacuate the casualties. So quickly we all loaded up on 7-tons and drove out Trash Road north of the city. And, as we dismounted the 7-tons, we immediately started taking sniper fire, which had never happened before. So, we got out, we secured the LZ, the company gunnery sergeant came driving up with two casualties from CAAT Blue. We got the bird [helo] in, popped some smoke, got the bird in, got the casualties out, and we waited for follow-on orders. We were told to extract the Recon OP, that had killed the fire team-size mujahideen [element], at the intersection of East End and Market. We loaded back up in 7-tons and continued at that location, and started taking some sniper fire upon arrival. We extracted the OP site, and then occupied the Baath Party headquarters and former police station. Inside the Baath Party headquarters, we discovered small arms of all kinds. Russian .50 cals, medium machine guns, AK 47s, RPGs, more than you can count. Big stockpile of weapons there, for a fight."

"I think that when our Recon OP ambushed the four guys, that were in the Baath Party headquarters, it tipped off their location, and the OP started taking fire, and that was when CAAT Blue came in, CAAT Blue lit up the Baath Party headquarters so much that whoever was in there just dropped what they had and ran. It's the modus operandi of the enemy in our zone to establish weapons caches in their chosen fighting positions and then move among them unarmed. Because they're aware of our TTPs—we will not shoot an unarmed individual. If they carry the RPG across town, of course we're gonna gun 'em down, but instead they stash them and move amongst the positions, where they can play off their center of gravity, being the fact that we can't distinguish them from 'Joe Average Husaybah'."

His Marines occupied the Baath Party headquarters and gathered up the weapons. CAAT took the weapons away, and Lieutenant Watson's platoon remained there along with the company gunnery sergeant. He learned that Lima 4 was now heavily engaged at the hospital east of their position. Watson was then ordered to move his platoon and link up with Lima 4.

"I pulled in our guys from the police station who had just returned from searching the kill zone from the Recon ambush, and found four enemy KIA. Pulled them in, platoon column, 300, 400 meters to Lima 4's position. Were not engaged, between the Baath Party headquarters and their location at the school just east of the hospital. We arrive there, and I immediately made link-up with Lima 4 Actual [platoon commander], Lieutenant [Dan] Carroll. And he was standing on the roof of a building, and there was a courtyard of a school, and then immediately east of that there was a building. He was standing on the roof with several other Marines. Some Marines were on the deck, with gun trucks leaning into the building, and I had no idea what was going on, absolutely no situational awareness at that point other than that I knew they had gotten engaged.

"And Lieutenant Carroll shouted down to me, 'Okay, okay, I need your guys to go around the building, and set up this AT 4 shot, this AT 4 shot.' I said, 'Hang on Dan, where's the enemy?' And then he kinda figured out what my awareness level was like, and stomped his feet on the roof and he said, 'They're about five meters underneath!'"

Lieutenant Watson continued intently recounting the events: "So here was the situation: He was on top of the roof of a building, that had five mujahideen fighters inside. And, he had half of his platoon surrounding it, to the west side of the building, and nothing on the east side. I sent a squad around to cordon off the east side of the building. Almost right after he stomped his feet," Watson snapped his fingers at this point, "Almost right after, a burst of AK 47 fire came outta one of the windows of the house. And their platoon sergeant, Sergeant Champion, was on one of the gun trucks, with a 240, and he musta put at least 75 rounds of seven-six-two [7.62mm] right into that window. And that was when I knew I just walked into something.

"So, I'm still talking to Lieutenant Carroll on the roof, and he says, 'How many AT4s do you have?' Hang on, hang on, you know, is there any chance that we can, you know, capture these guys?" Stepping out of his narrative for a moment, Watson remarked to me that human intelligence is so important out here: "You can't find the enemy with radar, you have to find them with Humint."

He then returned to recounting the events of that day, asking Lieutenant Carroll, "Is there any chance we can capture these guys?"

"He says, 'Brad, I lost four guys today.'"

"And I said: 'Dan, I got six AT4s.'"

Watson paused before continuing.

"I said, 'I've got six AT4s.' At that point, there was no way we were gonna take these guys captive. A couple more times they, you could hear them say 'Allahu Akbar', and there was fire through the windows, and we returned in kind from the gun trucks. I set up two AT4 shots into the building, maybe 25 meters northwest of the house we where had 'em trapped, and then two to the south. Meanwhile, Lieutenant Carroll, part of his platoon's still top of the building." Watson paused again, controlling his thoughts and emotions.

"Our whole idea was to put them in a kinda combined arms dilemma where they couldn't stay inside of the building, couldn't come out of the building. And he devised this whole plan, kind of meticulously put guys in place, such poise; Dan had such poise that day, with everything that happened. I put my guys in positions, said, 'Dan, how can I support you?' I put my guys in positions he suggested, they took their shots. Dan, actually I think was still on the roof, still on the roof when we shot the AT4s into the building ... with his Marines.

"The enemy didn't come out, so, we start thinking, what else can we do? What else can we do? Do we have any SMAWs? Yeah, we have to wait for it to come all the way from Camp Husaybah. That didn't work out. And then I'm walkin' over to Sergeant Champion, platoon sergeant, I'm about to say, 'Do we have any gasoline?' And we could hear Lieutenant Carroll call down from the roof, 'Hey, get some jerry cans!' So we handed up a bunch of jerry cans filled with gasoline to the roof. And he was up there with some guys from Recon. And they dumped all this gasoline down this staircase in the building. They dumped all this gas in, and when they [enemy] saw all this gas comin' in, they started firing from the building."

Watson said that Lieutenant Carroll came down from the roof with his Marines, and they threw some incendiary grenades into the building.

"He and I personally threw in a frag grenade through the window we'd been taking fire from. Cooked it off and threw it in, window, maybe about 10 feet off the ground. Jumped up and threw it in. It exploded and the blaze was ignited. Black smoke started pouring outta the house. We had it cordoned off so whoever was gonna run outta there to escape the flames wasn't gonna make it. Two guys tried. And both were, one was gunned downed by my 1st Squad who I had sent around to the east side of the building; the entire squad engaged one guy running out. Killed him.

"A second guy started running, on the west side, my SAW gunner, my fire team leader who had taken the AT4 shots from the side, had his SAW gunner set up to kill any enemy [that] tried to escape. The SAW malfunctioned, the fire team leader picked up his M16, put about half the magazine into the guy running out of the building. So at that point we'd killed two, we didn't know how many more were inside.

"Recon went in, after the flames went out, and cleared the building. It was, I guess, about a squad-size Recon element. Cleared the building, killed three more fighters inside, who somehow had endured that blaze. And then, quickly extracted because they saw a propane tank that was on fire."

Lieutenant Watson said that they waited for the fire to die down, and then Lima 4 went back in to collect their guys who had been killed in the courtyard. Three of their Marines were killed in the courtyard, and then Watson saw an M16 get passed out of the window as the house was being cleared. He said, "Earlier in the day, we'd all been talking on the radio as the company will, it was peculiar that we hadn't heard Lima 6, Major Gannon, over the hook [radio net] the entire day. Strange. Kind of in the back of your mind, like, 'Where's Captain Gannon, where's Captain Cannon.'[1] And, Lima 5 [the XO]

---

1   Captain and major were both used as ranks for Rich Gannon. He was a captain at the time of his death, and was posthumously awarded the rank of major. Lima Company's Marines used both terms when speaking about him.

came over the hook to me, just before we dumped the gas, and said, 'Hey, 3, this is 5. Have eyes on Lima 6 right now?' I said, no.

"And then I asked some of the guys around me, or if they'd seen him all day. They said they hadn't seen him since that morning.

"I was like, that's a negative, Lima 5, we haven't seen him."

"Was like, 'Roger, that, if you see him, let me know.' Okay, good to go."

At that point some of the Marines thought that perhaps Major Gannon had been captured. But then as Recon and Lima 4 were clearing the house, they passed out the M16.

"It was just a regular M16, A4, no ACOG, no special attachments, which these days is pretty much just carried by officers, staff and officers. So at that point I'm concerned, I shout for them to start reading off the serial number. They do, and before I can ask Lima CP if that serial number belongs to the CO, Lima 6, I hear Lieutenant Carroll come over the net and say, 'Lima CP, Lima CP, this is Lima 4. The CO is a routine.' And immediately, I thought, good, maybe he has minor injuries! Then I remember that [routine] also means KIA."

"So, inside that building, was the body of Captain Gannon. Discovered by Lima 4. Along with three other Marines that died trying to make entry, before I arrived on the scene. Okay, at that point, Lima 5 came over the hook and said, 'Roger that,' and just picked up and kept going. He said, 'My new call sign is Lima 6, stand by for follow-on orders.' We kinda broke the cordon, brought everybody back in. Lima 4 and I heard several different things. By now, the battalion QRF is on its way into Husaybah because the city has broken out into a city-wide battle.

"We received reports over the net from Humint sources that there were 350 mujahideen, foreign fighters, or enemy combatants, better word, in town, at a grid near our Firm Base. At this point we're all the way across town. So we have our Firm Base, a 350 enemy-strong force, is between us and our Firm Base. The battalion commander's convoy has arrived in town, they brought everything they could. At that point we didn't have any armor assets, so the biggest vehicle we had with our force was an up-armored Humvee with a TOW on it, and some Cobras, had Cobras."

Lieutenant Watson's platoon moved to the new police station for link-up with the battalion force, but when he and his men reached there, they received a Frag Order to move to the battalion assembly area at the intersection of Market and East End. To move that distance while under fire quickly, Lieutenant Watson "borrowed" Iraqi police cars, passing Lima 4 along the way. Watson walked up to Lieutenant Colonel Lopez's vehicle and the colonel told him about the attacks that were to be launched across the city.

Lieutenant Colonel Lopez said, "Where's Lima 6?"

Watson responded, "Sir, he's dead, sir."

Watson said that it was awkward; he didn't know how to say it. "Sir, he died."

Lopez asked, "How do you know?"

Watson replied, "We saw him at the house we were just at."

The colonel said, "Okay."

Then Lopez asked, "How many enemy dead?"

"Five."

"How many Marines?"

"Five."

Watson said that Lieutenant Colonel Lopez then wrote the name "Rick" on his map, and the numbers 5 and 5. Next, he began to brief Watson on a battalion minus assault through the city. It was to be a 31-block, house-to-house fight, from east to west, all the way back to the Lima Company Firm Base on the western edge of Husaybah, on the border with Syria.

"Lima 4 and 1, Lima 4 and Lima 3, were going to be tasked with the six blocks south of Market Street, which included the suspected enemy location. Force Recon was gonna sweep north of Market, and I think Kilo Company was south of us. So we received a Frag O, and went back to brief our squad leaders."

He said that helos came in low over the city, and enemy fire "lit up", right where the infantry was headed. "You could hear 'em shooting at the helos. The helos would turn sharply and head north to avoid the fire. So we knew we were goin' into something. We were supposed to cross the line of departure no later than 17:15, and go firm at the eight three gridline before making the final push into Camp Husaybah. The limit of advance was West End Avenue."

Lieutenant Watson and Lima 4 (Lieutenant Carroll) subdivided the six blocks south of Market Street. Lieutenant Carroll took Market and two and three blocks south and Lieutenant Watson took four, five and six blocks south. Watson put one squad for each block.

"And at 17:15 we got on line, as a battalion, and began to push. Blade 3, Major Schreffler, had come over the net, and said that ROE was the enemy was wearing red headdresses and black clothing. By this time, people had figured out, in the city, it was a city-wide battle; anybody who didn't mean any harm was hiding in their home with their family. So for the most part, anyone on the street, given their, sort of, modus operandi, moving among weapons caches, was considered enemy.

"And so, my three squads, along with Lima 4's three squads, got on line with the rest of the battalion and we began to push, at 17:15, for those 31 blocks. Along the way, my first squad was heavily engaged, probably encountered eight or so enemy defensive positions, and just sequentially took them all down, and kept pushing from east to west across the city. The squad I was with, 3rd Squad and later 2nd Squad, I was with 2nd and then 3rd, saw maybe two or three each, took 'em out, kept goin'. We went firm at the eight three gridline, inside a house with a family, and waited for the rest of the battalion to catch up."

Lieutenant Watson pointed out the control measures on the wall map next to him. He said that they "went firm" there and were told not to go any further west because the battalion's air assets were going to be engaging targets of opportunity in front of them. Watson's platoon was actually about 75 meters beyond that point, but he felt that his Marines were okay in their positions. He said that you could hear all kinds of aviation asset that day, both fixed wing and helo. The forward air controller told him there actually was just about every type of airframe in the U.S. military flying over the city. Watson said it had an incredible psychological effect on the enemy, with the level of combat power we could call on if we needed it.

"So at the eight three gridline, I distinctly remember having fixed wing on station, and that was very comforting to know we had the close air support that we needed. Right before darkness, I was hoping we'd stay at the eight three gridline 'til darkness fell, so we could put on our night vision equipment and have that advantage on the enemy before we pushed on to the limit of advance at West End Avenue. Around dusk we received the order to push. We went all the way from the eight three gridline to the limit of advance, and were not engaged. Which was surprising, because that was to be the most densely populated enemy resistance. We arrived at West End Avenue, and we were supposed to go firm there, and wait for the rest of the battalion to catch up. They didn't want to leave us just out in the open, so they took us across the Phase Line, occupied a building maybe 150, 200 meters the other side of the street, and then kept 'eyes on' our portion of the city: Those fourth, fifth, and sixth blocks south."

The day was exhausting for his platoon, so now Lieutenant Watson put two squads down (allowed them to rest) and had the other squad post security on that building they were in. It was now about 2100, and Watson listened to the radio net for instructions. He said that the instructions were pretty much coming from Blade 3 (Battalion Operations Officer) and Blade 6 (Battalion Commander). Kilo Company was assigned to relieve his position, and they did this at about 2300. Bradley's platoon was to go to Camp Husaybah after the relief, and prepare for follow-on operations on the next morning, April 18. Kilo Company and Weapons Company would continue to man the cordon of the city during the night so that enemy fighters could not escape. Watson's platoon could rest a little and refit during this time.

Lieutenant Watson said that his platoon got back to Camp Husaybah, he got some rest, and the next morning got up and prepared for another battalion sweep through the city.

"Eighteenth April we got nearly all the way through our lane, which was a couple streets west of the Baath Party headquarters, going from Trash Road all the way to Route Train. We were using doughnut charges to blow locks off doors to make dynamic entries, and searching *every* house, *every* person in the city. To be certain that we'd eliminated all the enemy inside the city. About four or five blocks before we reach our limit of advance, Route Train, we hit three weapons caches simultaneously. All within 10, 15 minutes of each other, my squad leaders would get me on the radio, and say 'Sir, we just found weapons caches!'"

"I would say we hit a pocket, where the enemy was storing their guns. We found all kind of things in there, too: RPG warheads, an old LAAW [Light Anti Armor Weapon] rocket, anti-tank rockets, AK 47s, some HKS assault rifle I'd never seen before. All kinds of different kinds of stuff, left in white bags in vacant houses. They obviously got outta there in a hurry, didn't bring their weapons with them. We confiscated all of those, and my former platoon sergeant, Staff Sergeant Wilder, got me on comm, and said, 'Sir, I need you to come over here and check this out.' He had just spoken with a man in one of the houses and asked him where the mujahideen, and it's common in Husaybah, for, when you ask people to say where are the mujahideen, they're so frightened, of the mujahideen, they'll tell you, 'Oh, we don't know, we have no idea where they are.'

"This man actually said, 'They're right next door.' I said, Roger that, they're right next door."

"We went next door and found three military-age males. At that point, I made link-up with my platoon sergeant, we brought our HET team in, start questioning these guys, and while they're being questioned, I distinctly remember my 3rd Squad dragging out belts of seven six two [7.62] ammo out of the house. As these guys are denying the fact they have weapons in their homes, we discovered a weapons cache underneath a pile of hay behind the house."

The Marines confiscated the weapons and later returned to Camp Husaybah.

They continued to question the men. There were also two women in the house, who were harboring anti-coalition forces. Lieutenant Watson got permission to detain the women, also. These women were later released, solely because they were female, according to Watson.

Watson then said that they did not take contact again until May 1. There was a period of significant stability between April 21 and May 1, not a single IED contact in the town of Husaybah.

On May 1, his platoon was tasked with a raid operation at the intersection of Market Street and East End Street. The ICDC had reported that the mujahideen was having a meeting every Saturday at 16:30 in an area with metal shops, a restaurant, and a carpenter shop. Watson and his platoon went in 7-ton trucks with elements from CAAT platoon. They dismounted about 300 meters from the target area. When they dismounted, an IED went off and blew off three tires from the 7-ton truck, causing six casualties among the Marines. There were three priority and three routine medevacs. CAAT vehicles brought the wounded back to Camp Husaybah.

"I lost so many Marines from the search element at that point I couldn't go full cordon and search the building. So I called for React. As I was calling for React, I started taking small arms fire from the opposite side of the street, about two minutes after. It seems as though in this town, they'll detonate the IED and they wait a couple minutes before they use the small arms. It doesn't make any sense, because we're the most vulnerable when we're carrying wounded off the streets."

This was the platoon's sixth IED attack, and it reacted quickly. CAAT vehicles started firing into the building, Lieutenant Watson called for an AT4 shot, and put an AT4 into the building. React got there and made a dynamic entry into the house, finding some spent brass, but no shooter.

"We hold the cordon, the React squad comes through, we take 24 detainees out of this building. Tag 'em, and transport 'em, transport 'em all back to Camp Husaybah, to be sent to FOB Al Qaim. We brought the dogs through and everything. The dogs, this is a suspected IED preparation location, this building, and one of the dogs had a hit for explosives inside the house, inside the building. Okay, we had the detainees, we had the probable cause, they had a little bit of evidence outta the dogs."

Then Watson and his Marines headed back to Camp Husaybah, and that has been the last contact they've had until the present.

Since then, his platoon has been tasked with running the border checkpoint with Syria. This checkpoint has been frequently mortared in the first two and a half months that they have been here. Also, there is always the vehicle-borne IED threat. The platoon still conducts nighttime patrols.

I then asked him how the Marines in his platoon have been responding to all that has happened to them. Lieutenant Watson responded: "It's very difficult for them. We came here with 42, due to casualties; at one point we had as little as 33 in the platoon. It was very difficult for them, and a week or so following that peak in enemy activity. But, you know, in keeping with tradition, no one complained, no one quit."

Watson again paused, then continued, "They say that you shouldn't fall in love with your platoon, I don't think anybody really means that."

HM3 Justin Thomas Purviance, USN
Senior Line Corpsman, Lima Company, 3/7

Casualties began from the first day that Lima Company arrived in Husaybah, but as Doc Purviance relates, the worst days came in mid-April.

"My career started off May 31, 2001, I entered RTC Great Lakes, graduated August 3rd, and from there I entered Naval Hospital Corps School. Spent 18 weeks learning how to do everything medical in my field. From there I went to Camp LeJeune, North Carolina, where I went through basic Field Med Service School to become a Navy 404 Corpsman, which is the Corpsman which serves with the Marine Corps."

He was then ordered to report to 3/7, 1st Marine Division, at 29 Palms, California on March 20, 2002. He said that he expected to serve some time on board Navy ships, but in his heart of hearts, wanted to serve with the Marines.

"Growin' up, I've always wanted to be a Navy Corpsman. Me and my little brother talked about both bein' Navy-Marine Corps team.

He's now a Marine with 1st LAR, and I'm a Hospital Corpsman with Third Battalion, Seventh Marines."

Doc Purviance was here in Iraq for about eight months in 2003. 3/7 moved from Kuwait through Safwan, all the way up to Baghdad. He saw few casualties, and most of the casualties he saw were Iraqi civilians. They then went to Karbala, Iraq, where they conducted stabilization operations, with projects like rebuilding schools. The battalion returned to the U.S. with plans to rest, refit, and began the training cycle again. But events in Iraq overtook this and the battalion began to prepare to return to Iraq.

Currently there are five other Navy Corpsmen that support Lima Company, one with each rifle platoon, and two with Weapons Platoon. All but one of them were here in Iraq last year.

He outlined current operations. "We arrived in Kuwait, waited for our gear to get here, waited for the rest of the battalion to catch up, waited on a C130 flight to come up here. We left Kuwait, roughly March 1st, to come occupy our area right here in Husaybah, right here on the Syrian border."

They flew up to Al Assad in C130s, then overnighted in CH53s up to Camp Al Qaim. After three days there, they moved up to Camp Husaybah in Army Bradley fighting vehicles. Two platoons and a headquarters element came to start building up the Firm Base. After joint patrols with Army units, the Marines took tactical control of the AO on March 14. Lima 3 (3rd Platoon of Lima Company) took contact on its first patrol in the city.

Doc (nickname for any Navy Corpsman) Purviance said that on about March 15 or 16, the first casualties came in, and for a while, there were casualties every day. The numbers went anywhere from four to 12 in a day, with wounds caused by anti-tank mines, IEDs, sporadic small arms fire, and grenades.

Doc Purviance often referred to his log to check on dates of events. On March 17, he said there were casualties caused by an anti-tank mine. "Resulted in the first two KIAs here. One of my junior Corpsmen in CAAT Red, and a Corpsman senior to myself, worked on six casualties, two of which were critically injured, one being PFC Smith, who we had to perform CPR on, for in excess of 30 minutes. Who ended up not surviving. He was pretty much killed instantly. And PFC Morris, who actually died later of his wounds, in a minefield."

Purviance said that a gun truck was driving in a minefield, and hit an anti-tank mine. The blast ejected the turret gunner about 50 meters, and the mine was directly under where PFC Smith was sitting. He took the direct blast from the explosion. One of the junior Corpsmen was injured by this blast.

"April the 8th was the day we that took the most casualties in one day. Resulted in one KIA, the death of Corporal Wasser. I believe we sustained 12 casualties that day, in an hour period. From IEDs. Corpsmen out there, they did exactly what we're trained to do. They didn't freak out, they didn't hesitate, they just, IEDs are still goin' off, and the Corpsmen on the ground are actually runnin' through the blast to get to these guys. To get them life support they needed. That was probably one of the worst days. The worst day of all, the 17th."

He said that April 14 through 17 were the three worst days they have had since they've been here. On the 17th they lost five Marines (KIA), including the Lima Company commander, Captain Gannon. Doc Purviance knew four of the Marines personally. Doc said that his Corpsmen did their best to treat the wounded, get them to him so he could get them on the birds and get them home to their families.

He said that most times during a medevac here, there are Army medics on the Blackhawks that evacuate the wounded, so the Navy Corpsman remains with the Marine unit on the ground when they turn the WIAs over to the flight medics.

"We sustain them to the point where they can make the 10- or 15-minute flight from here to Al Qaim, and then they get over there to the FRSS and the STP, which we got, ER doctors, trauma doctors, orthopedic surgeon, and they can start workin' their magic there and from there they're evacked to the next echelon, be it Al Assad, Baghdad, or Germany."

The Army Blackhawk helos have been on call for the Marines of 3/7 throughout the entire deployment. He said that it only took the birds 10 minutes to get to Husaybah, and often times when a ground vehicle was bringing casualties to an LZ, a bird was flying over as the ground vehicle was arriving.

I asked him to detail examples of things that the company's Corpsmen have done, that he could point to and say, "This saved a Marine's life."

He responded, "We initiated one casualty, Lance Corporal Fala, Colonel Lopez's actual translator and bodyguard. He received a gunshot wound to his left bicep, severing his brachial artery. HM2 Close, myself, and HM3 Bennet, we worked together, used Quick Clot, pressure dressing tourniquet to stop the bleeding enough to get him to Al Qaim to where the doctors could actually stent it and save the arm, save him from bleeding to death."

He said that many times Corpsmen have applied tourniquets to stop arterial bleeding and stabilize the casualties.

"On the 8th, we actually had Marines lose their appendages, or parts of their appendages, fingers, parts of a hand, and we were able to save a Marine's life and get him outta here before anything else could happen. Chest tubes, performing chest seals. We actually had a casualty, had a piece of shrapnel, chunk of wood stuck in behind his ear, stabilizing it to insure there's no further damage or any possible damage to the brain stem, or any damage to his ear.

"The stuff they teach you in Corps School and Field Med, and the stuff that I even thought when I first got here that I'd never do or see. Same thing with my guys. Stuff that they learned about and practiced on mannequins, we actually had to do live, in a real situation. They fared pretty well. They did exactly what they needed to do."

I then asked him about the casualties in 2003. He said that most of the casualties suffered by his Marines were minor things, like scrapes or frag wounds from mortar rounds. Most of those treated then were Iraqi civilians wounded in cross fire or from failing to stop at roadblocks. He even treated sick Iraqi infants. This year there was very little treatment of Iraqi civilians other than a few who were wounded in cross fire in Husaybah, and Iraqis who the Marines detained for questioning.

The preparations for this deployment included talk the possibility of providing some limited care for the Iraqi civilians if possible. But the way the deployment has unfolded, most of the treatment has been for wounded Marines.

We began to review the big day of fighting on April 17. Purviance said it began with a mortar barrage of about 25 rounds, and he stayed with the Lima Company COC here at Camp Husaybah with the XO (then-Lieutenant Dominique Neal), the first sergeant, and the gunny. Lima Company's QRF—Weapons Platoon—was then sent out, and "Pretty much all hell broke loose."

At about 16:30, Captain Neal, the first sergeant, the gunny and Doc Purviance attached themselves to Kilo 1 and went through the 440 area to the target house, receiving lots of gunfire en route. His junior Corpsman had to do a CASEVAC from out there.

"We were out there for about eight hours, towards the end of the evening, towards the end of the fighting, to bring in the rest of the battalion's effort to get the other guys who had already been fighting all day, to cordon off the city. Hopefully stop any will to fight of the 'freedom fighters'."

Doc Purviance said that he had had a little bit of training with mortars, and he helped to get the base plates set up for the 60mm mortars in case they were needed to shoot.

In conclusion he said, "I think I kind of underestimated what we were comin' into this year. Last year it was, you know, we were buddies with the Iraqi people, we were friends. We'd sit down with them, drink tea, you know, have chicken. Lot of time we weren't even walkin' around the town in battle gear. And to come into it [this year] and watch a lot of the guys I've served with for the past three years, injured, having to treat them, knowin' that their life was in my hands due [to] the situation here. I just think, myself, personally, [I] underestimated what we were comin' into. I don't think it affected the way I did my job, or my Corpsmen's job for that matter."

Captain Dominique Baissou Neal
Commanding Officer, Lima Company, 3/7

Captain Dominique Neal was XO of Lima Company during the heavy fighting in Husaybah (April 17–19). The interview started off routinely, and then became very emotional as he recounted the operations on the day that the former commanding officer, Captain Rich Gannon, died in combat operations, and then-Lieutenant Neal had to run the company for most of the day from the CP at Camp Husaybah.

We met in a windowless room, with a large map of Husaybah under plastic covering a table in the middle of the room. For the next hour and 12 minutes, I would listen to a story that ranged from the routine preparations for deployment up to the day that Captain Neal was thrust into his current billet when Captain Richard Gannon was killed in action.

Captain Neal graduated from the U.S. Naval Academy, and attended TBS and IOC (Infantry Officers Course) at Quantico before joining 3/7 in November 2000. He served as a rifle platoon commander for 18 months. In May 2002 he became the assistant operations officer for the battalion (S3 Alpha), and served in this billet throughout OIF I. During the SASO portion of OIF I, he became the executive officer (XO) for Lima Company. On return to the U.S., he extended to serve as company XO again for this deployment.

"We had just gotten back from OIF I, September 4, spent about two weeks doing the reconstitution of the, all the battalion accounts, most closely, my company account. Then we went on a 30-day leave block. I remember talking to my family, being asked if we were gonna go back there, 'cause the Army seemed like it's gonna get committed for a much longer period of time. I said there's no way. Marine Corps, we open the door, we don't stay in the house. We just open the door and let the Army occupy it."

When Neal came back from leave, the company commander Captain Rich Gannon said to him, "You'll never guess what's going

(Left) Lance Corporal Jonathon David Stamper, USMC. 3rd Squad Leader, 3rd Platoon, Kilo Company, 3/7. (Official Photo by LtCol David E. Kelly, USMC, Ret.)

(Right) Lance Corporal Brian Matthew Schultz, USMC. SAW Gunner, 4th Platoon, Kilo Company, 3/7. (Official Photo by LtCol David E. Kelly, USMC, Ret.)

(Left) Colonel Craig A. Tucker, USMC. Commanding officer, Regimental Combat Team 7 (RCT 7). (Official Photo by LtCol David E. Kelly, USMC, Ret.)

(Right) Lieutenant Colonel David E. Kelly, USMC, Retired. (Author's personal photograph)

Border crossing between Husaybah, Iraq, and Syria. (Author's personal photograph)

Captain Dominique Baissou Neal, USMC. Commanding Officer, Lima Company, 3/7. (Official Photo by LtCol David E. Kelly, USMC, Ret.)

First Sergeant Michael John Templeton, USMC. Company First Sergeant, Kilo Company, 3/7. (Official Photo by LtCol David E. Kelly, USMC, Ret.)

Lance Corporal Daniel Rene Johnston, USMC. Team Leader, 2nd Squad, 1st Platoon, Lima Company, 3/7. (Official Photo by LtCol David E. Kelly, USMC, Ret.)

Lieutenant Bradley Ryan Watson, USMC. 3rd Platoon Commander, Lima Company, 3/7 (Official Photo by LtCol David E. Kelly, USMC, Ret.)

HM3 Justin Thomas Purviance, USN. Senior Line Corpsman, Lima Company, 3/7. (Official Photo by LtCol David E. Kelly, USMC, Ret.)

A Marine NCO conducts pre-convoy brief for trip to Husaybah, outside of the headquarters of 3rd Battalion, 7th Marine Regiment at Camp Al Qaim, Iraq. (Author's personal photograph)

Author in watch tower overlooking border crossing area between Syria and Iraq at Husaybah. (Author's personal photograph)

(Left) Squad Leader Corporal Jason Lemcke points out FOB Husaybah/Camp Gannon at the western edge of the city of Husaybah, Iraq, right on the border with Syria. (Official Photo by LtCol David E. Kelly, USMC, Ret.)

(Right) Corporal Jason Alan Lemcke, USMC. Squad Leader, 3rd Squad, 1st Platoon, Kilo Company, 3/7, attached to Lima Company, 3/7. (Official Photo by LtCol David E. Kelly, USMC, Ret.)

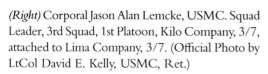

Lance Corporal Jerad Duane Allen, USMC. Military Policeman, 2nd Platoon, Charlie Company Military Police, attached to 3/7. (Official Photo by LtCol David E. Kelly, USMC, Ret.)

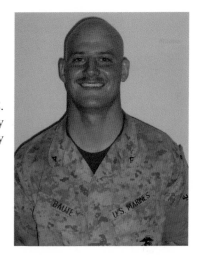

Lance Corporal Daniel Patrick Baute, USMC. Military Policeman, 2nd Platoon, Charlie Company Military Police, attached to 3/7. (Official Photo by LtCol David E. Kelly, USMC, Ret.)

Corporal Christopher Logan Cahill, USMC. Motor T (Transport) Operator, Truck Platoon, 1st MHG (Marine Headquarters Group). (Official Photo by LtCol David E. Kelly, USMC, Ret.)

Gunnery Sergeant Brian Wayne Eyestone, USMC. Platoon Sergeant, 5th Platoon, 1st Force Reconnaissance Company. (Official Photo by LtCol David E. Kelly, USMC, Ret.)

Corporal Michael Thomas Phillips, USMC. Combat Engineer, 1st Combat Engineer Battalion, attached to 3/7. (Official Photo by LtCol David E. Kelly, USMC, Ret.)

Staff Sergeant Ronnie Lee King, USMC. Platoon Sergeant, Military Police Platoon, Charlie Company, attached to 3/7 (Official Photo by LtCol David E. Kelly, USMC, Ret.)

Corporal Kristopher Elliot Benson, USMC. CAAT Section Leader, Weapons Company, 3/7. (Official Photo by LtCol David E. Kelly, USMC, Ret.)

Captain Bradford Wilson Tippett, USMC. Commanding Officer, India Company, 3/7. (Official Photo by LtCol David E. Kelly, USMC, Ret.)

Staff Sergeant Alexander Anthony Carlson, USMC. Platoon Sergeant, 3rd Platoon, India Company, 3/7. (Official Photo by LtCol David E. Kelly, USMC, Ret.)

Lieutenant Colonel Matthew Allen Lopez, USMC. Commanding Officer, 3rd Battalion, 7th Marine Regiment 3/7. (Official Photo by LtCol David E. Kelly, USMC, Ret.)

Commander Edward William Hessel, MD, USN. Officer in Charge of Shock Trauma Platoon (STP) 4. (Official Photo by LtCol David E. Kelly, USMC, Ret.)

Lance Corporal Jason Alan Sanders, USMC. Platoon Radio Operator and Mortar Section Leader, 4th Platoon, Kilo Company, 3/7. (Official Photo by LtCol David E. Kelly, USMC, Ret.)

Corporal Ryan David Griffey, Weapons Instructor and Gunner, Truck Platoon, MHG, attached to 3/7. (Official Photo by LtCol David E. Kelly, USMC, Ret.)

to happen. We might be goin' back." Neal said, "I just kinda laughed. Sure enough, we got the word that we're going back."

"The AO was unconfirmed, but in the meantime, we started doing the prep work." This included getting all accounts updated, closing any gaps in supply of gear and weapons, and building on small unit leadership. They went to live-fire ranges, re-BZOed their weapons, and started SASO training.

1/7 hosted the division's SASO training, and the battalion continued with SASO training of its own. After Christmas break, they did another division training package at March Air Force Base. "We had a target date on which the battalion could do set-level training for actual buildup." By late November, Lima Company knew that it was to be the main effort of 3/7 when it returned to Iraq. Captain Gannon was the most senior company commander in 3/7, with the most resident knowledge on SASO operations. "We were very well-organized, very methodical." Neal felt that Lieutenant Colonel Lopez had a lot of faith in the ability of Lima Company to operate out in Husaybah, relatively remote from the battalion.

About the deployment, Neal said, "Real interesting. Skipper [Gannon] and I had a long talk beforehand. There was an advance party that was goin' out and the colonel [Lieutenant Colonel Lopez] basically had a spot on where to go."

He said that often, Lieutenant Colonel Lopez would pull Captain Gannon away to see how Lieutenant Neal would do. As an example, he said that during a training operation, Gannon came down with the flu, and Neal ran the company in the field. When Gannon tried to return after a day, Lieutenant Colonel Lopez told him to go and rest with his family. Similarly, when it came time to send out the advance party to Kuwait, Lieutenant Colonel Lopez decided to send Lieutenant Neal in this group along with the company gunnery sergeant. This also gave Captain Gannon another four or five days to spend with his family back in the States. Captain Neal expected to be in Al Qaim about three or four days for a leader's recon before the rest of Lima Company arrived at Al Qaim. But when Captain

Gannon and the company arrived in Kuwait, he decided to go directly to Al Qaim, and then-Lieutenant Neal took over the preparations to move the company into Iraq.

The rest of the battalion convoyed up into Iraq, while Lima Company and H&S Company flew up to Al Assad and then to Al Qaim. Captain Neal was the senior Marine for this air movement. He admitted to being surprised at being entrusted with so much responsibility. It was a much more decentralized command structure than the previous year's deployment for OIF I. When he got to Al Qaim he expected about a week before moving to Husaybah, but Captain Gannon met him and told him to be ready to leave in three days.

"I thought we were going to move into the Baath Party headquarters, we ended up moving out here close to the border. The original notion was not to be near the border complex 'cause it just got mortared all the time." Neal said that once they got to the Baath Party headquarters, he could see it was not a tenable position; the current company position was actually better able to be secured. Also, many key elements were in place nearby: The ICDC headquarters, Customs police, border complex buildings, and vision on the Syrian border. Captain Neal said that his knowledge of Husaybah came from some satellite imagery, and some PowerPoint Intel presentations.

The Firm Base here did not have any walls around it, but there was good stand-off distance from the city proper, as well as an open area between it and Syria.

Captain Neal said that Captain Gannon had used him as an operations officer in addition to being the officer in charge of administrative and logistics affairs. This additional trust and responsibility helped Neal to develop experience with company tactical affairs. Gannon told him, "No, you're gonna be an Ops O and an XO."

The Marines built up seven-foot-high HESCO barrier walls around the camp, strung up concertina wire, built two towers to overlook the city, and constructed a live-fire range. But the buildings did not have hardened roofs, they were still mostly sheet metal roofs, and Captain Neal wanted to have better overhead protection for his Marines. He said it was tough to imagine how "non-permissive" the environment would be.

The company received incoming mortar fire their first night at the camp. When Marine engineers came to the camp, they were unable to build overhead protection, but worked "24-7" to get the wire strung and the barriers built. He also said that at critical times, the battalion commander or regimental commanders visited while the camp received mortar fire.

Captain Neal said that due to its isolation, the company operated almost like a battalion. "In order for us to sustain out here, one company organic, can't do it alone. So it required, one company with the Weapons Platoon to become a provisional rifle platoon, so it's four platoons right there. On top of that, we have another CAAT team [with TOWs, .50 caliber machine guns, Mark 19 machine guns, and 81mm mortars], which was originally CAAT Red, which became CAAT Blue because it sustained casualties."

Kilo Company provided two additional rifle platoons, Kilo 1 and Kilo 4, although Kilo 4 got pulled out later. They also had a Forward Air Controller (FAC) Team that included an officer and radio operator, two sections from STA platoon, a Recon platoon in direct support, a section of AAVs and occasional support from a platoon of tanks for several days at a time. He also had 60mm and 81mm mortars set up.

"We were doing heavy saturation patrolling when we first got here. We did a Left-seat, Right-seat with the First of the Third ACR, about 10 days." Most of this patrolling was mounted on the Bradleys. Captain Neal said that after the relief of the Army on March 13, 2004, the Marines took out their first mounted patrol and had their first contact. For about the next four weeks, each of the platoons began to run at least three patrols a day for heavy saturation of Husaybah. That would be about 15 to 16 patrols a day, both mounted and dismounted, emanating from Lima's Firm Base. One platoon would provide force protection at the base. To the enemy, there seemed to be no set pattern to the patrols. After this initial surge of patrols, the company cut back on the number sent out because platoon commanders were getting worn out.

The method of dismounted patrolling was different from the Army's mounted patrols in Husaybah. It was a deliberate effort to show the people the human face of the Marines in their city. "Eventually, we thought the presence in the city was very warm, after they got used to seeing us on the ground, talking to people, realizing that you take away all that armor and all that padding, there's just people with flak and Kevlar. We felt it was friendly enough we could go down to platoon minus, eventually down to squad-size patrols, which is what we did in Karbala."

He said that things began to change in mid-April: "We started getting a very lukewarm feeling. The IEDs were still there early on, but they were outside the city more or less, not with CAAT Red. CAAT Red took a significant amount of casualties." CAAT Red was doing border patrols and patrols south of the city.

"We received some single-source Intel that the mujh [mujahideen] was going to do [an] anti-coalition propaganda effort, and really try and hit us hard, and establish their credibility and try and demoralize us, so we went back up to platoon-size patrols." The source said that this would happen over a three-day period starting around April 8. So Lima Company planned to again saturate the area with patrols. Captain Neal said that this was the first time he saw single-source Intel that turned out to be accurate. "3rd Platoon took some pretty good IED attacks." 1st Platoon had two satellite patrols out that hit IEDs and had Marines who required medevacs. They were pushing to get a medevac for badly wounded Lance Corporal Wasser, when word came over the net that the medevac had just become routine. This meant that Wasser was KIA. The same day, Lieutenant Watson took an IED hit and had to be medevacked. "It wasn't demoralizing but definitely an eye-opener."

The company went to eight-hour patrols for each platoon. This did not mean walking constantly for the eight hours on patrol. During these patrols, three platoons would establish OPs, do VCPs, staying out in the city for eight hours. Neal explained to his platoon commanders that these patrols were out there to deter enemy activity and learn what was happening in the city. "So that's what we did. We had another attack on the 14th. Even on the 14th we sustained a few more casualties. Kilo took one." Captain Neal said that when they were doing the four-hour patrols, if they hit an IED, the patrol had to cordon off the area, wait for EOD to destroy the IED, and there might be another patrol coming in the meantime. With the eight-hour schedule, the time for an IED event did not affect the time of the patrol as much.

There were three different contacts on the 14th: One hit Kilo Company, one hit the battalion commander (Lieutenant Colonel Lopez), and one hit Lima Company.

"Then the 17th came." Captain Neal said they were "making their money" at night between the 14th and the 17th. They were finding IED makers, and bringing in suspects for HET interrogation. Weapons Platoon had returned from a patrol, got chow and hit the rack (gone to sleep). The CO and Captain Neal had a good rotation going between them: Captain Gannon worked the days and Neal the nights. The company had now closed down the border crossing.

"17th I had been up all night, I said I was gonna let Captain Gannon sleep a little more. He was definitely a perfectionist because he cared so much about the Marines. Very methodical, very critical, very analytical on what he wanted to do." Neal said that when Captain Gannon gave his commander's intent, he was always very careful to explain it.

"Then we got the 25 mortar barrage out here [pointing on the map] at the border checkpoint. He's [Captain Gannon's] up, because our normal battle drill is, we take indirect [fire], everyone goes flak and Kevlar, we get accountability, see everyone's okay. There's OPs 'cause you're not gonna go out and chase a mortar man down, you're not gonna catch them."

Recon was out in the city, saw some fire, and stirred up a hornet's nest. They started firing on the mujahideen immediately, and the enemy started firing back. Lima sent out the company QRF. The QRF was the platoon that had just returned that morning. Coincidentally the battalion S3 (Major Schreffler) was here at the Firm Base, and would be here for the entire three days of these actions. Neal said it was either good timing or good karma to have him there. The S3 was talking to Battalion, Neal was talking to the company. "Right off the back, we hear an IED go off, it's hit by CAAT Blue. Same time, they're trying to figure out where Recon's fire is, so we can draw some of their fire and find where the enemy is and we can kill that." When

CAAT Blue hit that IED, they got hit with a barrage of 7.62 fire and RPGs coming right at them. Captain Neal said that the Humvee that was hit was currently outside his CP and had about 32 holes in it, and the windshield was almost completely shattered.

The company gunny went there along with Lima 6 (Captain Gannon). Lima 3 launched out to help provide a cordon around an LZ for a helo medevac. In the vicinity of a wadi (a ravine), CAAT was trying to get the casualty up along Trash Road to the LZ when they took contact. Meanwhile, Neal got word at the CP that Weapons Platoon had taken a casualty—a gunshot.

"But I do hear from Lima 6 because I hear, 'Hey, Lima 5 this is Lima 6, I got good news. The good news is we got three in surgeries, medevacked on the birds, they're outta there. The bad news is, we got a routine KIA in Weapons Platoon.' I say, roger that, sir. Haven't heard anything from Battalion yet, we're still reported up, I got 3 [S3] here. Is there anything you need on our end, sir? Just to let you know, I got Lima 3 out there, they established an LZ, need anything push in for support, they'll push in and reinforce ya, so they're there, and I got another platoon standin' by, if you need support, you got both Kilo 1, Lima 2, you need additional force."

Gannon responded "Hey, roger that, all right, I'm goin' off with 3."

Neal said, "That was the last time I heard from Captain Gannon. Normally, when he's out there, more times than one I'll hear Captain Gannon on the net. A lot. I mean, a lot. Not only because he's micromanaging, because he's just, I can't see in the CP, as the Ops O. I can see units on the map, and bein' in the 3 shop before, you learn to visualize more than anything. But, the more information's fed to you, the more you visualize. Well, he goes off freq, I'm hearing information getting crossed between the two, and I'm calling back from the CP, not trying to really step on the 6. Anytime the company commander goes forward, he really becomes the COC, I'm just kinda getting information called back."

Captain Neal was listening to sitreps from units out in town, and the fight went on. Then a few hours had gone by and no one had heard from the 6.

Lima 4 linked up with Lima 3 and Broadsword (call sign for the Battalion S3 officer) at a building where they had some insurgents holed up. Captain Neal learned that Lima 4 took three more casualties. Lima had been in a fight all day, and Battalion was moving in to support them. Lima 4 and Lima 3 needed ammo resupply. Captain Neal wanted to get SMAW ammo, AT4 rounds, 7.62 and 5.56 ammo up to this building.

It seemed that every Marine unit in the town was getting hit, and still no one had heard from Lima 6. Captain Neal said that Marines in Lima 1 and Lima 2 at the Firm Base were eager to launch out and join the fight, but he didn't want to send too much so he'd have someone back there for the next fight. He told the platoon commanders to keep their guys out of the sun, and if he needed them he would call them.

Lieutenant Colonel Lopez got on the net and said that he could resupply the two platoons, just have them take out the building. Plans were still in flux. Captain Neal talked to Major Schreffler and told him that he still had no comm with Captain Gannon (Lima 6).

Neal continued: "I'm gettin' concerned about him now. I haven't heard from him, no one has. The 3 [3rd Platoon] hasn't heard from him, the 4 [4th Platoon] hasn't heard from him, Broadsword hasn't had any word on him, CAAT hasn't seen him, and I'm just getting that sinkin' feeling in my stomach that something's not right. Wishful thinking, though, that maybe he got shot, or maybe something happened, but he's, like, maybe in a corner. Maybe he's not necessarily in that building, but he's just in a building with no comm, he's just hunkered down, hoping that we'll take out that building and then we'll link up and grab him. Guys, you know, sometimes people get separated."

Marines know their rally point, and they can get there, Neal was hoping.

"Recon and Lima 4 come up with a plan where they torch the building, they get appropriate fuel tanks, throw it on the building, and throw a flare on there [actually, in his interview, Lieutenant Watson of 3rd Platoon said that they used grenades to ignite the fuel in the building], or pyro, plan on smoke 'em out. After the building dies down, they shoot all the enemy there out of the building. They find out that, in the process of recovering the three Marines from Weapons Platoon, in the vicinity of that building, finally a call on the net, back from Lima 4. Says, 'Hey, found the 6, Lima 6, is routine.' So I'm like, wow. Your initial reaction is you want to say, well, put him on the hook [radio handset] then, I'm tryin' to speak to him all day, thinking routine is routine injury. You know, maybe he was just hurtin', couldn't get to a position where he could say where he was.

"Then, reality starts setting in a little bit. He's gone.

"So, you say the one thing that you never, ever want to say in your whole life. Especially, you know, you may do it at TBS, you do it at IOC. You may do it in a trainer. Even though, it's more of a … in training you do it, it's more of a competitive thing, because you want to do well. It's more of a pride thing. Not that you … you just don't foresee it. I don't think there's been anything like it since maybe Beirut, or maybe in Vietnam."

"But you say it."

"You say it: All stations on net, be advised, be advised, Lima 5 is now Lima 6.

"Everyone says. 'Roger'.

"At that point, I become Lima 6. And, even though you're just focusing on Ops, it just gnaws at the back of your head. It just gnaws you. It gnaws you at the back of the head. You just lost your company commander, you want to finish the mission, get the boys back, repeat, restart, and go ahead. Let's finish this thing out. Get a fresh start. That's when you actually look to see the SPC come out of the woods and say, 'Okay, let's recock this and start again, do something right.' The truth is, the Marines were doing everything right, that's just the realities of war. But at the same time you just replay over and over again, what could you have done better?"

Now that he was running the company, Captain Neal continued to focus on the fight, and knew that he had to get Captain Gannon back to Camp Husaybah as soon as possible. "At that point, another single-source Intel comes in, says, 'Hey, there's a CP down south that needs to get hit. I think it's the insurgents' CP. Battalion wants you to go ahead and destroy it. And we got guys on mujh hot line, there are mujh holed up in that house right now, so speed. And they're mujh movin' in, trying to take space.'"

He said that there were rumors that the ICDC had turned on the Marines, but he later learned that this was not the case.

Major Schreffler told Captain Neal to take the rest of the two platoons, minus the force protection element, and go destroy the house. Neal wanted to finish the first fight before taking on this new fight, but the major's order was clear. So Neal took out his map, and formulated a plan. He brought his platoon commanders in, and told them there was a "target of opportunity" there, an enemy CP house, and the two platoons had been tasked with attacking and destroying this house. One platoon would be the point platoon and the other the assault platoon.

"Three or four years ago, Major Schreffler had of come up and told that to me, I probably woulda blown a gasket." Neal credited the command experiences that Captain Gannon had given him with his being able to react quickly now, in this storm of activity.

Captain Neal was told to expect casualties right out of the gate. He said he didn't want to hear this after losing four Marines and his company commander. "I want to hear, we're gonna go out there. We're gonna smash these guys, we're gonna come back. We're gonna reset. We're gonna debrief this, find out what coulda been done better, go forth and execute."

Major Schreffler asked him what his Cas Plan (casualty evacuation) was, and he replied, "Sir, I got one TOW vehicle and a 7-ton."

He continued, "So we bring that out there, and literally, not even 10 minutes out the gate, 2nd Platoon takes three casualties." Due to the battalion sweep that started in the east of Husaybah and was moving towards the west, everything that was in the city was now moving towards the southwest part of the city, near Neal and his Marines.

Neal was launching the medevac back to Camp Husaybah when an RPG round hit the 7-ton and busted the fuel tank. "Doesn't go off, though. So the 7-ton limps back out along with the TOW vehicle. We try sending birds to 2nd Platoon to pull those three urgents, urgent casualties out of there, but the LZ's too hot. I want Kilo 1, the assault element going into the CP, the enemy headquarters. We're pushing to get into position to reinforce 2nd Platoon, at least by fire."

While he was doing this, 2nd Platoon was drawing fire, but from a new direction, an area north of them. His 2nd Platoon commander called for fire from the 81mm mortars, and Neal remarked, "A lotta good things going on that day. The first round went right into the enemy CP, and destroyed it. The same time, while we're doing that, we finally got the Cobras and Hueys to come in and strafe the target. And that really put a hurtin' on them, along with the M guns [machine guns] shooting at 'em in the vicinity of the radio tower. So the Hueys came in real low, and destroyed that. Blackhawks weren't gonna come back and pick us up in that LZ that was previously hot. But it bought us enough time, and neutralized the enemy to a point where we could get another 7-ton vehicle back out and take the casualties back.

"We finally move in, Kilo 1 and I finally get into position. Kilo 1 took two AT4 shots into the building, and destroyed the building. Finished it. We got there, linked up with 2nd Platoon. 2nd Platoon established a cordon. We moved in, cleared out, actually got some mujh guys. That was the building where the HQ was, burning to a crisp. Whoever was in there was pretty much ash. Finally finished up, headed back to the CP, where [on] the 18th we did a company sweep, north to south. Actually, a battalion sweep, we had east of the city. Actually found a lot of remnants of heavy activity. Lotta [weapons] caches, lotta RPGs. Some detainees that we ended up pulling from the hospital, mujh. Also, some guys who were being harbored inside the city. That there, moving through the city, made the company feel a helluva lot better, because it showed that we did fight well that day. We did make an impact with all the stuff we got. Look at what we actually have to fight within the city, look at how much damage we did to the mujh effort. 'Cause in the end, we ended up getting two guys that harbored a significant amount of ammo: RPGs, RPG rounds, RPG launchers, RPK, AK 47, and all that stuff."

At the time, Neal was still a first lieutenant, and then assumed that the events of the 17th and 18th were done; eventually a more senior officer would replace him as company commander. He said to Lieutenant Carroll that he and Carroll were the only officers who could talk to the company and, "I don't know who's gonna be our company commander, but we're going to trust him, but the Marines are gonna need someone to talk to before they get to know this company commander." However, Lieutenant Colonel Lopez came down and told Lieutenant Neal that, "Hey, we're going to frock you, make you company commander, we'll go from there."

In the month after that, the company got out of 24-hour wearing of flak and Kevlar on the camp. Neal started a rotation of his platoons back to Camp Al Qaim for rest and refit periods, and went to less than platoon-size patrols (after approval from the battalion commander and battalion operations officer). Captain Neal had the capabilities of having STA, Recon, and CAAT elements out in town in addition to his infantry assets.

The local population has gotten more friendly towards the Marines since April 18. Shops have reopened. There has not been an urgent, life-threatening casualty in Husaybah since April 18. Currently two platoons provide patrols, with one platoon doing two patrols and the other platoon doing one patrol a day. CAAT also does three patrols a day. One platoon provides camp security, and one platoon is permanently on the border checkpoint. Captain Neal says that it is a sustainable operation. "If you walk around and see the Marines, the morale is up, they like being here, they like what they do. They've seen the results based on, literally, blood, sweat and tears, a lot of heart, a lot of effort, a lot of tenacity on the 17th. And they're now reaping some of the benefits."

Captain Neal said that it's gotten to the point that he has to force platoons to go up to Camp Al Qaim for rest and refit, because if there's a fight in Husaybah, his Marines don't want to miss out on it. "They don't want to relax away from us." But Neal knows that it is important for his Marines to be able to step back for a short time and just relax.

Captain Neal said that he hoped that Major Piedmont and I would be able to get back out to the camp and meet with more of his Marines, perhaps go out on patrol with them. He knew Captain Christopher M. Kennedy, a field historian who had been out with Lima Company last year. Captain Kennedy had also been a close friend of Major Gannon.

When speaking of his Marines, Captain Neal said, "It's a great bunch of guys. You have 18, 19-year-olds that are, honestly, when I see the work ethic, with can-do attitudes, it's amazing."

He had one platoon commander who is a Staff NCO, two platoons with sergeants serving in the platoon sergeant billets (a Staff NCO's job), and squad leaders who were very young corporals.

"They're going out here and making decisions. When you hear them give an Op Order brief, it's funny, because you go to TBS, and you remember back in your TBS years, how you hear your fellow peers stumble through an Op Order. But you got guys who are 18 years old, at TBS, all you have to work with is just your organic platoon, and you just give them a simple Op Order. These guys, they have attachments, they know how to call for fire, they know how to call, do CAS [close air support], they know how to call an on-line medevac. They have all this responsibility on them, and they come in, they come in and do their overlay, they do a brief and the brief is clean in like 15, 20 minutes. You're amazed. You're amazed, you gotta come back here and see this. Only way I can show you is link up with one of these squad leaders, or one of these platoon commanders and just see it for yourself."

He said that even though the fight was very political, there was a strong, vital leadership circle between the platoon commanders and his squad leaders. This young officer had successfully assumed command during trying conditions, and continued to calmly lead his rifle company.

★ ★ ★

The facilities at Camp Husaybah were austere—makeshift sleeping areas in what seemed to be old warehouses, and an area to park Humvees and 5-tons tactically to minimize damage from the sporadic mortar attacks on the camp. Heated meals were delivered from Camp

Al Qaim. All of the buildings were constructed of cement blocks with metal roofs and brown stucco outer walls; Marines had light-proofed windows with old MRE cases taped to the glass. Sand-filled HESCO barriers had been constructed by combat engineers to give protection from small arms fire formed the boundaries of the camp that faced Syria. Many of these barriers had the slogan "Complacency kills" spray painted on them. Syria lay about 200 meters away across a stretch of trash-strewn brown sand.

My interview sessions at the camp were done, and I waited with Major Piedmont for Lieutenant Colonel Lopez to complete his tour of the tiny camp on the Syrian border crossing. Lopez was assessing the condition of the Marines at the austere outpost by meeting with all levels of the company. We soon boarded our convoy's Humvees, left the front gate and drove through Husaybah back to Camp Al Qaim.

CHAPTER 4

Marines of Kilo Company

Wednesday June 2, 2004: Camp Al Qaim

By mid-afternoon, Major Piedmont and I got back to Al Qaim by convoy, and found more Marines waiting for us to interview them. The ride back was still a little nerve-wracking, but we now had learned that the threat here had decreased significantly in recent weeks. We both just hoped that this would continue. We drove out of the camp, and went south towards the railroad tracks on the outskirts of the city. Then we continued out towards the main camp at Al Qaim. This command (3/7) was very concerned about getting the stories recorded and had us overbooked for interviews again. So there was little downtime for either of us. Major Piedmont asked them to lighten the schedule (which they did), and it looked like we would have to try to get out there again in the near future. (Note—we never did get to return to this area.)

First Sergeant Michael John Templeton
Company First Sergeant, Kilo Company, 3/7

This interview lasted over an hour. Captain Neal's interview had also been an hour and 12 minutes. I did not think that this was due to my developing interview skills. Rather, it was that I was meeting more of the Marines on the "tip of the spear" out here in Husaybah.

First Sergeant Templeton went to Sea School after recruit training, and served on the USS *Simon Lake* as part of the Marine detachment for three years. After getting married and reenlisting for three more years, he went to Hawaii where he was assigned to 3/3. On his next reenlistment he went to become a drill instructor at Parris Island. Around this time the Gulf War kicked up, and he wanted to go to the war; however, his orders sent him to the Drill Field. After two years there, he returned to 3/3 where he served in a variety of infantry billets. He later served as assistant Marine officer instructor (MOI) at the University of Ohio. He eventually became Kilo Company's first sergeant after he joined 3/7 at 29 Palms.

During OIF I he was with Headquarters Company, 7th Marines, as their Career Planner. He said, "There wasn't too much career planning going on. I was assigned to the S1, and one of our biggest chores was pretty much the escort for the regimental commander on the march up." He was in one of the lead vehicles during the march up from Kuwait into Baghdad. On the second day of the war, they had crossed the border, he guessed somewhere near Basrah. The S3 told him that there was a problem in an area where numbers of Iraqi tanks and armored vehicles had been disabled. As friendly forces approached the vehicles to search them, enemy fighters would appear from nearby. His seven-man patrol of Marines gathered up some 64 enemy fighters, despite some sniper fire.

Once in Baghdad, he was involved in escorting VIPs, because he was riding in a gun vehicle (with a .50 cal machine gun). He returned from Iraq in June 2003.

In December 2003, he was selected for promotion to first sergeant, and was "frocked" as first sergeant for Kilo Company, where he began work in January 2004.

"We had a high number of people returning for a second trip here. I know within the battalion it seemed we had a lot of new first sergeants, some of the Staff NCOs were relatively new. We were fortunate enough to have 70 percent of people coming back here for OIF II, veterans of OIF I."

First Sergeant Templeton came into Iraq from Kuwait along with the main body of 3/7. He said that the Army was glad to see the Marines show up, "They couldn't get out of here fast enough. They suffered a lot of casualties." The Army had Bradley fighting vehicles, which were much better armored than the up-armored Humvees that the Marines brought.

"We went and did two weeks with the 1st of the 3rd, going out on patrols with them, from Al Qaim all the way up into Husaybah. Back and forth within the Bradleys. Bradleys, I think the Marines became very comfortable inside them, maybe too comfortable." He felt that the Marines are much more adept, however, at boots-in-the streets presence, compared with the Army approach of patrolling in the Bradleys.

Once the Army left, "I want to say the first couple of weeks was pretty hairy." The Marines had gotten used to riding in the Bradleys, and now they would have to ride in high-back trucks with sand bags on the floors and partial armor on the sides, and some up-armored Humvees.

"We had a few vehicles early in March that hit mines or IEDs, causing considerable damage to the vehicles, wounded a few of the Marines, and it was a shocker." First Sergeant Templeton said that the Marines expected to take some damage, but the damage caused by the IEDs was greater than they anticipated. He said that now they are having many fewer injuries and a lot less damage to the vehicles. He doesn't know if this is due to greater vigilance by the Marines in discovering the IEDs, or the enemy just getting sloppier in their use. He said that since the middle of April, there has been a considerable slowdown in these IED attacks.

Around the beginning of April, starting April 9, it seemed that the whole country of Iraq had a wave of attacks. At the time, the Marines in Al Qaim thought that it was just in this region. Later, they found out that it was in many parts of the country.

"We had one of our patrols, I think it was 4th Platoon, 1st Squad. It was in north Sada, which is one of the first cities we had come to out of Camp Al Qaim on our way to Husaybah. I was involved with a unit, CAAT White 1, and Kilo 3rd Platoon. We had a squad of Marines who we had taken out to the city of Karabilah. It was a 12-man squad, had four vehicles, two up-armored vehicles, one with a TOW mount, one with a Mark 19, and then we had two high backs. As we got to Karabilah, the boys from 3rd Platoon, about the time they were dismounting the vehicles, we had heard that 4th Platoon and CAAT White 2 had encountered an IED as well as some small arms fire. We dropped off the dismounted squad so they could conduct their patrol, a presence patrol, is what they're doing. The patrol leader, Staff Sergeant Lott, got on the radio and asked if they needed assistance."

The night attack took place north of Sada, on Route Diamond. As the four vehicles that Templeton was with approached the fighting, they took small arms fire. SOP at the time called for the Marine vehicles to turn into the fire and gain fire supremacy. As the Marines dismounted and returned fire, they started to take small arms, RPK, and RPG fire.

"We got hit with probably about 12 RPGs on the west end of Sada." The Marines got into their vehicles to move about 100 meters, closer to Route Jade. Lance Corporal Atrain, who was in the fourth vehicle, started to engage with his 240 Golf machine gun. An RPG then hit the rear quarter panel of First Sergeant Templeton's Humvee, but the driver could not get out because the door jammed. Templeton got out on his side and ran around to the driver's side, which was under enemy fire.

"For the most part, we couldn't see the enemy, only muzzle flashes." Another RPG hit the rear of a Humvee, knocking Templeton to his butt. He said at the time he was laughing about it! Then another RPG round went off around the fourth Marine vehicle. This wounded Lance Corporal Atrain with shrapnel. "I stopped laughing. It was reality."

They pushed another 100 meters in the vehicles, and received similar enemy resistance. First Sergeant Templeton said that at about this point, they were receiving fire in Sada from the east end, the west end and from up front.

"I was guessing there was at least 60 to 100 people out there firing at us. We pushed one more time and got in the middle of Sada, by this time we'd covered about 500 meters. That was about the fourth or fifth time we stopped. An RPK had opened up on a, the, rear vehicle."

An RPG round bounced, flipped over, and hit Templeton's Humvee. It was flaming up but had not yet exploded. The driver of the fourth vehicle had leapfrogged ahead to avoid shrapnel from the round. An enemy machine gun raked the fourth vehicle: Machine gun rounds went through the TOW tube, rendering it useless, and more rounds went through the sights of the TOW, hitting the gunner in the left arm and knocking his NVGs from his face, and his GPS device from his chest. The driver was also hit. RPG rounds were also exploding underneath the vehicles, and Staff Sergeant Lott decided to move the vehicles out of the kill zone. The total time of this fighting was about 20 minutes.

Templeton estimated that Lance Corporal Atrain put about 3,500 rounds of ammo through his machine gun during this action. They found out only later that while all of this was happening, Weapons Company was also being hit in Ubaydi.

First Sergeant Templeton said that one of the problems in this area near Sada is losing radio communications with the battalion. There is a large low-lying area, and radio transmissions out of there are difficult. When they got out of the kill zone, Templeton was yelling at Staff Sergeant Lott to get the battalion QRF out to them. Staff Sergeant Lott was always one step ahead, and had to switch radio frequencies to Lima Company's freq. Then CAAT Blue came on scene, provided security, and allowed the patrol itself to go and get its dismounted Marines that had been placed at Karabilah about an hour earlier. Once these Kilo Marines rejoined the patrol, CAAT Blue left and went to other fighting near Husaybah. "I just remember when CAAT Blue got on scene, it probably struck fear into the heart of the enemy. As they moved from west to east, there wasn't a shot fired at their vehicles as they went through what was just our kill zone." Templeton recalled that he could hear dogs barking in the distance, a sign that someone was moving through that area: "You could basically tell where they were, just from the rhythm of where the dogs barked."

He then said that the medevac was taking place. "We had a suspicion that Torres had been killed. As a matter of fact, Staff Sergeant Lott, he never said to the guys that he thought Torres had been killed as he pulled him out, and put him in the back of the vehicle. But as I went to see if I could help him, go from that particular part of the ambush as he was getting the vehicle ready by the column, and at that point he kinda whispered, 'I think that Torres is dead.' But he never said that loud enough for anybody else to hear. Had he said something, it would have just killed the morale of the guys there." Templeton felt that if the Marines thought that they were fighting for two wounded Marines they would have a little bit more fighting spirit.

First Sergeant Templeton said that it seemed that they waited for an hour for the medevac, but it was probably only about five minutes.

"As we were evacuating the casualties, we were searching all over for a wound on Torres. Never looked at his face. Went over his body, had him pretty much, his upper body stripped down. Looking at him, we couldn't tell if he had been hit. The birds got there, Atrain, he walked himself up, I escorted him over to the medevac bird as they were still trying to find wounds on Torres. I got him [Atrain] to the first bird, pretty much on his own, I just kinda held his hand, I guess, and got him, he was on his own. Then I went back and helped them with Torres. They landed the first bird, and I guess the first bird was pretty much the security bird. The second bird was actually the medevac bird. And we carried Torres to the first bird, got him on the bird, and they said, hey, you gotta take him off and put him on the other bird. And that was, for me, the worst part of the whole night, because there was still hope he was still alive. Still never found out where he got hit, we just knew that he wasn't talkin', and, we didn't have a Corpsman on the scene.

"I think maybe Staff Sergeant Lott, I was worried about the security and making sure everybody was where they needed to be, waiting for the counterattack, and Staff Sergeant Lott was taking care of the casualty, along with one of the other Marines in his vehicle. We carried him [Torres] to the bird, and at the second point we were exhausted, just carrying him from the firefight, carrying him that short distance to the bird. I ended up putting him in a fireman's carry and took him to the second bird. And the only thing going through my mind, I'm telling him, sorry, 'cause I'm hoping he's alive. And I'm just thinking if he's, if he was hit, if the bullet didn't kill him, me carrying him in the fireman's carry's gonna kill the poor guy. We got him onto the bird. That was kind of rough. You couldn't lay him down gently, it wasn't like the movies, everything didn't just fall in place. We had our difficulties getting him on the second bird before it lifted off."

Once he got back to Camp Al Qaim several hours later, First Sergeant Templeton learned that Torres had been killed by a machine gun bullet though his head. A Corpsman said that Torres had probably died instantly.

Templeton was initially upset about why the battalion had not sent out the QRF sooner. He later read the battalion log, and found out that the battalion staff did know that there was a firefight going on, but the fight it was aware of was the one that 4th Platoon of Kilo was having. The radio "dead space" prevented the signal from the Sada area from getting to Battalion, so Battalion did not know of their predicament. A lot of the QRF had gone up into Ubaydi for fighting there that night.

The next morning, two vehicles from CAAT White 1 went up to Sada to try and find out what had happened. All of the houses in Sada were empty! There were shell casings in some areas. Then busses pulled up with women and children and they began to reenter the houses along with their belongings.

About a month later, First Sergeant Templeton was in Sada on a dismounted patrol. His Marines were handing out soccer balls and talking to the inhabitants. Templeton spoke with the owner of the house where he had seen the two enemy firing on the night of the fight. The owner had papers saying that he had been in custody that night and was not there for the fighting. But this Iraqi man had been told that three masked men had pulled up in motorcycles and went house-to-house in the town, telling everybody to leave their homes or they would be destroyed either by U.S. forces or by anti-coalition forces. The townspeople listened to this threat and vacated their homes.

But Templeton's opinion was that now these anti-coalition forces could not get away with this again, given what had happened in the area in early April. Also, the presence patrols by the Marines have established better relations with the locals. Many Iraqis have told the Marines that they are glad to have the Marines here, even though they will also probably be glad to see the Marines leave. The mujahideen had urged the locals to stand and fight in Husaybah, but the locals who did fight on April 17–18 saw that the many of the mujahideen deserted the fighting when it got too heavy.

First Sergeant Templeton also had recollections of Corporal Dunham, who was awarded the Congressional Medal of Honor for his actions in Husaybah. He said that Dunham was a great Marine. On April 13, Dunham had stayed up all night inside the COC working on his order for the next day's mission. "He had such respect from the guys in his squad. I remember him sitting down there, working on his order in the COC, and he had his fire team leaders, this was about, after midnight. His fire team leaders went to the chow hall for midrats, came back and gave him a plate of chow. That's, they were that tight. His squad loved that guy. He was just a great squad leader."

On April 17, the people of Husaybah were warned (by anti-coalition forces) to stay off the streets. Battalion had Intel reports of a number of foreign fighters that were supposed to be in the area. The exact number varied from 100 to several hundred. After the battalion swept through the city from east to west, on about April 19, Kilo 2 under Lieutenant Johnson sent foot mobile patrols into Husaybah. About two blocks into the city, he was met by a group of women who said that there were many people who needed medical attention as a result of the fighting.

Lieutenant Johnson called for Corpsmen from Camp Husaybah, and the women led them into a building with about 30 injured Iraqis there. The Corpsmen and Marines began to administer first aid to these people. 3/7 then sent in vehicles with more medical help, and evacuated some of the wounded for treatment back at Camp Al Qaim. Templeton related that the locals weren't mad at the Marines for the injuries, but were mad at the mujahideen for causing the fight. The women claimed that the mujahideen were cowards. Many of the women were grateful for the medical help given.

"We kind of changed the way we're doing things," he said. Kilo has two CAAT sections and three active rifle platoons. They often send out a full CAAT section (four vehicles) along with a platoon of Marines. There is also usually a full rifle platoon and full CAAT section operating out of Hill 212, south of Sada, which sends out patrols. This hill is manned round the clock. During IO operations, the force left there is sometimes smaller, but the position is always manned.

Templeton noted that from April 18 until the present, there has been minimal contact with the enemy, either with IEDs or firefights. In early April, many of the IEDs did not cause much damage. But in the past week or two, he said that the IED count has again gotten back up to the level of early April. Several vehicles have been badly damaged, but there have been few casualties.

In early March, Templeton said that many of the IEDs were made of bundled 155mm rounds, or remotely ignited rockets. Their intended targets were the Army Bradley fighting vehicles. He was in a Bradley in March, returning from a patrol, going through the town of Sada. A white dog crossed the road between two of the vehicles, then a remotely ignited rocket went off, hit the passenger-side turret, failed to detonate, and ricocheted off. When the Bradleys left, he said that the rocket attacks dropped off. However, the attack on Lieutenant Colonel Lopez's vehicle involved two remotely ignited rockets that were placed on both sides of the road. On April 20, the Marines apprehended a man that they designated the "Rocket Man."

One sign of an IED emplacement in some areas was a line of broken glass placed across a road. Templeton saw this for the first time after a mine had hit an up-armored Humvee in March. He was with a team responding to the attack, and saw the glass pieces placed on the road.

Since April 19, some of the IEDs are just hidden in burlap bags along the side of a road. There have also been some three-wheeled carts with multiple 155mm rounds found lately.

First Sergeant Templeton expected that when the U.S. turns over power to the Iraqis at the end of this month, that their presence patrols in the towns may be cut back, and more emphasis placed on convoy escort and route security. But he said that the higher-ups would make those decisions.

Lance Corporal Jonathon David Stamper
3rd Squad Leader, 3rd Platoon, Kilo Company, 3/7

I found the interview remarkable in that this young Marine did not refer to any notes; the events he described were all very clear in his mind. His squad was heavily involved in the mid-April fighting.

This young Marine has been with 3/7 since he finished his initial training. Lance Corporal Stamper enlisted in the Corps in 2001, graduating from recruit training in September 2001. He got sick at SOI with Strep throat and was sent to the hospital for surgery. He then returned and went through SOI again before reporting to 3/7 in March 2002. He has served in both OIF I and OIF II. There were only two platoons in the infantry company when he joined, with corporals and sergeants doing staff sergeant jobs. The company gradually built up to T/O and did MOUT training at abandoned housing at Edwards Air Force Base. After extensive training in late 2002 that included a CAX, he found that instead of going to Okinawa for deployment, the battalion would be going to Kuwait for OIF I.

Once in Kuwait, the battalion trained to attack Iraqi defenses. Living conditions were Spartan—no chow hall, no showers, and no air conditioning for the tents. 3/7 then moved close to the Iraqi border, and during the night got the word to tear down all of the gear for the move into Iraq. The next day they moved in Amtraks to just south of the border and staged there. During one of these days waiting for the attack, the codeword "Lightning," meaning a SCUD attack, was called. Then came the push north.

Stamper said, "The push north was long. We just stayed in Traks. We had a lot of people crammed in Traks." A machine gun squad was put on his Trak because theirs had broken down, and a detainee was also put on the Trak for a while. During the day they rode in the Traks, and stopped only at night, where they would dismount and dig skirmishers' trenches. A big sand storm stopped the movement for a while.

Nearing Baghdad, they stopped at a quarry, and dug what Stamper called a "very, very good defense." The Marines were there for two or three days, and launched constant security patrols. Just outside of Baghdad they were stopped, and had friendly artillery fire support through the night. As they prepared to enter Baghdad, they cammied up and got on the Traks, with music playing to get the Marines pumped. "We went into Baghdad and the Traks started lighting up this building as soon as we went in. I guess it was their company's objective to take this building. We saw two TOW missiles come streaming in, hit the top of this building."

The Marines dismounted and approached the 13-story building in order to search and clear. He thinks that it was the Ministry of Defense building.

"3rd Platoon went in from the right side, the 1st Platoon went in on the left. We went in, started clearing it out." This took some time, and they set in a defensive posture there. They ran patrols into the city from this Firm Base. "Everybody there they seemed really, really happy to see us, especially in Baghdad. People would come up and put flowers in your Kevlars, and just be thanking ya, hugging ya, giving you flowers." However, he added, "There was looters all over the place."

In about four or five days, Kilo Company was moved to a different section of Baghdad where they took over another building. At the first building, they had never taken fire. Here things were different: "Our squad was the first squad on patrol, and we went down the street maybe three, 400 meters, took sniper fire, from a building pretty far away. We moved towards it, tried to cordon it off, but by the time we got there, snipers had fled." After that there were no significant firefights. They did find many weapons caches in the city, including anti-aircraft missiles, mortar rounds, and AK 47s.

After they left Baghdad, that was the first day they got hot chow in the form of T-Rats (tray rations). They ate eggs, waffles, and other cooked items. Lance Corporal Stamper said it wasn't great, but they had been eating nothing but MREs for about a month at this point!

They pushed south to Karbala and set in at what used to be a school building. Each platoon had its own room and the company ran patrols. MPs set up a police training school, and Stamper's platoon sergeant got his Marines involved in helping to train the local police. One of the techniques was to teach the Iraqi policemen how to cuff unruly prisoners, as shown by some of the Marines.

Also, he said, "The Seabees that were there with us rebuilt some schools, painted 'em and stuff. We got to go out and help them sometimes. We'd go out for security and they wouldn't need everybody that they brought out there for security, so the people that weren't helped them rebuild schools."

While they were there, a lot of the senior non-commissioned leaders left the company, and Stamper got to act as one of the company armorers. A new commanding officer, Captain Gibson, took over around the end of June 2003. They began to take mortar fire, mostly on Thursday nights.

On August 1 they moved to the battalion log (logistics) site, and Kilo Company was responsible for area security. "The last night I was there, they dropped some mortars on us." He said that the mortars were walked right across the base.

It was a nine-hour drive south into Kuwait. They unwound for two weeks there, then returned to the U.S. In early September, the Marines received a 30-day block leave.

Lance Corporal Stamper continued, "The day of our [Marine Corps] Ball, November 10th, we found out we were coming back, the morning before the Ball. Our company commander told us, so, we found out we were coming back. Went to the Ball, and we had a great time at the Ball, and we went out this time and just started training."

The company did a lot of Lane Training and SASO training. After another leave period and some more training, they returned to Iraq. This time they convoyed up from Kuwait. "A lot of things were different. Kuwait was a whole lot nicer. We convoyed up. Right before we convoyed up, I got moved back into a line [infantry] platoon." Lance Corporal Stamper had been trying to get back into an infantry platoon from the time he learned that they would return to Iraq. A platoon needed a radio operator, and he had a lot of experience on the radio. Then Stamper was "traded" to Staff Sergeant Walker's platoon to be his radio operator.

Kilo Company had made a change in its organization for this deployment. It took its Weapons Platoon, and divided up the Marines so that it would have four rifle platoons with permanent weapon attachments. One platoon flew in, the other three rode up in unarmored vehicles, with a stop at Al Assad.

"We got up here, it was a lot different than we had anticipated. The base, they had a place that sold chicken. When we first got here they had a pizza shop, just right out front of this building."

The Army had allowed Iraqi merchants to set up these shops at Camp Al Qaim. There was no PX, and no chow hall either. Marines were eating T-Rats and the Army units were retrograding out.

The Army took out key leaders on joint patrols, showing how they operated in the area. These were primarily mechanized patrols, while the Marines intended to do primarily foot patrols.

"We did our first patrols out here in 7-tons. It was a platoon-sized op, we were supposed to move through what was nicknamed 'RPG Alley,' link up at this big open area nicknamed 'The Quad' out here." The Marines used satellite patrolling to confuse the enemy in the city. (On a satellite patrol, a unit splits into smaller patrols that go on independent routes, with a rendezvous point at the end of the patrolling.)

He said that Corporal Johnson, a squad leader in the platoon, came up with a method of providing some protection for the Marines riding in their Humvees: He got plywood, stacked it in the back of the vehicles, and put sandbags outside of this, as well as sandbags on the floors. They also built benches in the center of the vehicles so that they could face outboard and cover sectors better while riding along. The Humvees were not up-armored at that time, but this jury-rigged solution was better than riding with no protection.

Once they took over the camp, the Marines closed down the pizza shop and chicken store. Lance Corporal Stamper said that then, "We started getting a lot of face time in with the local people. Just doing a lot of dismounted patrols, just dismount and walk maybe four, five clicks. Satellite patrolling. Bringing our translators along." The Marines wore their green cammies when they first got here, and locals noticed the differences between them and the Army. The Marines walked in the towns, talked to people, and gave children candy.

His platoon was reorganized, and Lance Corporal Stamper became team leader in 3rd Squad. He described how they would do their nighttime patrols: The vehicles would drop off a patrol and then drive further on to conduct their own mounted patrols in other parts of the city. During one of the dismounted patrols, he was right behind the patrol's point man and they both saw tracer rounds being fired about 1,000 meters in the distance. The squad began to move by bounds towards these tracers. It turned out that these flashes were from an enemy firing at the mounted part of the patrol that had left them off in the city. The fighting ended before his patrol got on the scene. This mounted patrol had one of its Humvees hit by a dud RPG round.

Stamper said that the Humvees began to get better protection. First came improved Kevlar blankets for the floors, bolt-on steel plates for the sides and doors, and stable benches in the rear for seating.

"April 17th, word came down that there was a big uprising. The insurgents had broadcast in the city of Husaybah, any coalition forces seen in the city would be killed." It was also a warning to the civilians to stay off the streets. "We all loaded up, the whole battalion, pretty much, we moved out there. Our company, we got up there initially, Weapons [Platoon] was already up there, our CAAT vehicles, and they were taking fire. Right as our 7-ton was pulling up, an RPG screeched over the head of the southernmost vehicle. It was [the] north-south road, on the east side of the city."

His platoon dismounted and went back to insure that a house nearby was cleared. Lance Corporal Stamper went in with his squad leader and a few other Marines and cleared that house so that Marine snipers could set up in there for support as the Marines moved through the city.

"Soon as snipers got in there and got up on the roof, they started taking sniper fire, and it was pretty much whenever they were trying to put their heads up." He said that some of the incoming small arms fire was fairly accurate, hitting within a few feet of the Marines there.

"We all lined up, right as we were getting ready to push, some guy with an RPG came running up to the center of the street. And, my SAW gunner dove out in the street, and the .50 cal on the Humvee that was covering the street, was over his left shoulder. It was maybe four, five feet over his left shoulder. And he lit the guy up with his SAW, and the .50 cal started firing simultaneously. Then we started pushing down that street. It was the third street up from the south. And, our 3rd Squad was on the far south, we were the southernmost element to the company at that time. And our 2nd Squad was just adjacent to us, to our north. And our 1st was to the north of them."

"Started pushing, and we would push down one block, and, wait 'til the other squads got up on line with us. Well, it came across our radios, the only kind we had was PRRs, because it was so outstretched. Our platoon had higher comm, but as for each individual squad that wasn't with the platoon RO at the time, it was just PRRs, and Motorolas, to talk back and forth between the squads. Our platoon sergeant said, Staff Sergeant Walker, said they're coming up, our 2nd Squad was coming up on a wall, and they were gonna have to push one street south, and two blocks. So we divided the squad, and cover more ground. Help clear out that one alleyway to our south, so we could integrate into it as we pushed south. They split off and we were moving down the next block. And as we were movin' we heard an explosion over on their street. Didn't know what it was at the time, but later we found out there was some guys in a house, down at their street. The guys popped up on the roof, fired an RPG, and it actually went through the first two members of the team, and ricocheted, like skipped off the road, almost in between the second and fourth guy, as they were bumpin'. Threw a rock up, like, the rocket hit a rock on the road, and it skipped off of that, and threw the rock into our 203 gunner in the 2nd team's leg. Gave him a big bruise, and the rocket did continue down the street. It exploded on a house about a hundred meters behind them. So they got down behind a wall, and they took cover from the RPG around the corner of a building.

"And we heard the rocket go off, so we ran up and, it was just my team at the time. There were five of us, plus the squad leader with us, Lance Corporal Santos, and we saw the street. There was one alleyway we could go down, get to their alleyway, and right past that, maybe 50 meters, beyond the next house. There was another alleyway that pushed south, so Lance Corporal Santos took two of the Marines, was gonna try and come around and flank the enemy. And we were gonna go down and cut 'em off, so kinda catch 'em, so they could only run south of us, if they tried to run. And we pushed down, myself and Lance Corporal Torres, the 203 gunner in my team, he was on the left side of the road. I was on the right side. I ran up and got beside this orange and white truck, there was maybe a three-foot gap between that and the wall of the house. And the house that was directly to my right at that time was the house where they had gotten the RPG shot at 'em from, [but] I didn't know it, I didn't see it fired [earlier]. Directly in front of me there's a large house, had a wall around the roof. I could see bullets hittin' it from our gun trucks over on the East End street. So I was scanning it, and as I'm scanning it, there were, a gun truck said they saw eight guys on the roof of that house. And I saw two guys pop up, one of 'em, later we found out, he had the Dragunov and the other one had an RPK. And they started shootin' at me, I started returnin' fire at them. The way the wall was set up you couldn't see very much of their face, only like a four-inch disk on their face because of the cover from the wall."

Stamper continued to calmly recall the start of this firefight:

"So, I started firing at them. They're firing at me, and I heard the rounds slamming into the truck, like they're walking closer to me. It was kind of like you hear in a movie, like: 'duuu, duuu, duuuu, duuu'. Getting louder as they're coming toward me. And then the front windshield shattered out. And I was standing at the hood of the truck, and I saw a round go through the front windshield, and crack right by my head. So I took cover.

"My platoon sergeant ran across the alleyway, 'cause he saw me firing at the house to the south. And he got behind a little wall, was basically standing in a gate, it only covered like the front half of his body. He was about eight feet away from me. I turned, and I looked, and I was like, 'Staff Sergeant, they're up on the roof, they're firing on us, they got machine guns, you gotta get down.' And right as I was screamin' it, he, the machine gun burst came down and hit him, he got hit in the arm, the leg, his magazine took a round, his magazine caught on fire. And so, I turned around, screamed for my 203 gunner [40mm grenade launcher], to put rounds into the roof of the house. Right after he fired the first round, Staff Sergeant Walker pushed back across the alley and went runnin' down to, back to where our 2nd team was. And he went back down there."

Lance Corporal Stamper started to move from the front to the back of the truck, to try to get better cover and a better angle to shoot at the rooftop.

"The other half of my team came runnin' down the street, Lance Corporal Sanchez was up front. He had his ACOG, and he had eyes on the guy with the sniper rifle. And he was firin' his rifle at the guy while he was runnin'. And I just caught him through my peripheral vision, and one of the guys on the roof had thrown a grenade. And it went off a few feet in front of him, and I saw the wall behind him explode, and he collapsed. He was bleeding from both his arms, and he started crawlin' around the wall to my corner. And I reached over there and grabbed him. He was helpin' himself and I kinda helped pull him over and push him against the wall. Told him to check his self over, find out where he was bleeding from while he was still conscious. Make sure he was all right instead of patching himself up while we were still shooting at the house. He just looked down at his arms real quick, said, 'Naw, I'm good,' and jumped up.

"My SAW gunner came runnin' down the street and we didn't know it yet, but we were taking fire from the house where they shot the RPG from [earlier that day]. Those guys on the roof firing down at us, and guys at the one house where my staff sergeant had gotten shot from. There was a third house, kinda next to the house to our south. As my point man, he was movin' last to get to us, Lance Corporal Sanchez, myself, my SAW gunner Lance Corporal Villareal, he got shot from the third house, in the back of the leg. He went down in the street. So I went over, moved back over the front of the truck. My SAW gunner didn't know exactly where we were 'cause there was still a cloud of smoke from the grenade so he didn't know which direction to run. And he had run towards the house we were takin' contact from initially. We screamed at him and he heard us and started running down the street backwards, puttin' rounds at the house. Got back up to the front of the truck with me. [I] told my 203 gunner to keep puttin' rounds into the house. He shot all the rounds [40mm grenades] he had, and he came running over to the truck where we were, and I had extra rounds for him in my pocket. So he passed me his 203, and I was grabbin' his 203 and I started puttin' rounds into the house with the rounds I had.

"While that was happening, my squad leader, Lance Corporal Santos, Lance Corporal Torres, with my rifle, moved around and they went back into the street to get our point man, PFC Soscia-Chavez, he was still layin' in the street where he got shot in the leg. They grabbed him and were dragging him back to cover. As they were draggin' him, he was calling out 'Ah rats' to the third house that was firing at us, and still returning fire while he was getting drug away. Kept puttin' rounds on the house where the guys were. Drug him around, started workin' on him. We were still firin'.

"While down the street, our second team, while our first team's doing all this, a guy jumps out of a gate where they were and started throwin' frags at em. He threw, I think, three frags. First frag, actually, hit one of the guys' Kevlar and rolled down his back, and luckily all three of his frags were duds. They threw frags back over the wall at him."

Stamper said that there were also enemy fighters on the roof of that building. They also found out later that his team was getting fired on from this location. Lance Corporal Stamper ran down the street to this position to get more 203 rounds, and came back with about six of the 40mm rounds. Lance Corporal Santos was still shooting, and SAW gunner Lance Corporal Villareal was providing first aid to PFC Soscia-Chavez. Villareal was also an assault gunner, and told Stamper that he wanted to fire a round on the house. Stamper gave him the go-ahead.

"He passed me his SAW, and I started suppressing for him. He jumped out in the street and fired a rocket at the house and hit the wall right where one of the guys had been shootin' at us up on the roof. Blew a hole through the wall, obviously. And that pretty much, after that rocket shot, they slowed their fires down a lot from that house. Our squad leader, Lance Corporal Santos, ran down that street, to the other team, grabbed an AT4 from them and came running back. Fired that into the same house, and pretty much, null and voided the fire from that house. My assault man, Lance Corporal Villareal ran back out into the street with his SMAW again, put a round into the second house that PFC Soscia-Chavez had been firing at.

"After all that happened, I grabbed Lance Corporal Villareal and myself, kicked open a gate of the house right there, this was the house where they fired the initial RPG at. Went in there, cleared that house out, there was maybe 10 people in there, four males. We got them collected up in there, cleared it out, went up on the roof, came back down and got our wounded in there. A Corpsman from the CAAT vehicles and another sergeant had pushed down to our contact. The Corpsman came in, with their staff sergeant, Staff Sergeant Walker, and Lance Corporal Santos, and they started treating their casualties. I got all of the guys to come up on the roof. We set up security there until the medevac could take place."

After the wounded Marines were medevacked, Lance Corporal Stamper and his team went down from the building and continued to push into the city. At this point they were only three blocks into the city. He estimated that the firefight had lasted about a half hour, and it was a total of about three hours from when they began the entry into the city until the medevac took place.

Once the medevac was done, Stamper acted as squad leader, and he reorganized the squad to continue the push. The CAAT vehicles pushed south and put up a base of fire on the houses that were shooting at the Marines. The squad then went in to search the house. The house that had held the eight enemy had one dead on the roof, the wall on the roof was about five feet high, and provided good cover for firing down on the Marines. But there were three holes in the wall where the rockets had punched through, and Lance Corporal Stamper felt that these had surely caused the enemy casualties. After the Marines entered a second house, an RPG was fired at one of the CAAT vehicles. They arrested seven suspects in this house. By this time it was about 2200, and it was dark.

The squad then pushed south, leading the gun trucks by about 100 meters. The gun trucks drove with lights out. If the trucks drew fire, the Marines on the ground would be close to the shooters. "So we pushed down to the other end of the city, linked up with the platoon commander and our guide, who had become our platoon sergeant, because the platoon sergeant was injured. Stayed in their house that night. We set up, provided the western edge of the cordon, just puttin' guys on watch on rooftops. The word was still out, any military-age male comes outside, and engage."

During the night, Lance Corporal Stamper talked with the platoon commander. He was told that he'd stay as squad leader for the time being.

The next morning, the platoon commander sent him on a short patrol into the town. Then the platoon went into Camp Husaybah after the second day was over. They had chow there, and rested for a few hours. Stamper then went to a platoon brief for a potential mission: To go to the Husaybah-Karabilah (HK) triangle between the two towns and cordon off the area. The mission was cancelled as the weather got bad, preventing air assets from being able to provide air medevacs. Instead, the platoon returned to Camp Al Qaim.

Things have gotten significantly quieter since April 18 for this squad. "Since then, we've done two patrol bases, one 96-hour where we went up to Karabilah and occupied a water treatment plant that had been under construction. We occupied that."

They have also run joint patrols with the Iraqi police to help train them up. The platoon has also sent out local security patrols. Stamper clocked one of these patrols on his GPS: "I tracked on my GPS. During the 96 hours we were there, my squad walked 73 miles on local security patrols." These were to prevent rocket or mortar attacks on the camp.

At another water treatment plant site, they went for a six-day patrol base in the HK triangle. It was broken down into 48 hours on local security, 48 hours on patrols with the police, and 48 hours on guard post. This was quiet.

Current SOP requires that their vehicles must be within 200 meters of them when inside the city. Stamper said that this helps operations, in that medevacs and fire support are better available, but the Marines lose the element of surprise as the vehicles make noise as they travel. Kilo Company has a rotation for its platoons out of Camp Al Qaim. One platoon at a time goes to a patrol base on Hill 212 for 48 hours, running patrols and providing a React force. Things have been quiet there lately.

Lance Corporal Brian Matthew Schultz
SAW Gunner, 4th Platoon, Kilo Company, 3/7

Lance Corporal Schultz, like many other Marines over here, has kept a personal journal so that he can remember the events he participated in. It has helped me immensely when I speak with them, since their thoughts and memories are well organized. His squad set up a VCP (Vehicle Check Point) near the arches on the main road into Husaybah during the mid-April fight.

A year ago this Marine was at MCRD, San Diego, in the middle of his recruit training. He began training on June 24, 2003. He completed SOI at Camp Pendleton on 12 December, and joined Kilo Company, 3/7.

Schultz began, "At the time, there were three platoons and a Weapons Platoon, and I was in the 1st Platoon." In the two months before the move to Iraq, the company trained to prepare. He said that a lot of the company was new, and the training was good.

He said that when the company got to Kuwait, it did an "NFL type draft" to decide how the company would be reorganized into four infantry platoons. The platoon commanders and platoon sergeants picked their squad leaders, and from there more picks were made. (I did not get a chance to confirm this process with the company commander.) That meant that now there were mortar men, SAW gunners, and assault gunners in each platoon.

"Which is kinda nice, too, because when we're out there and we need a SMAW, then we got that assault man who carries the SMAW and knows everything about it so he can apply it. Same thing with machine guns. If he needs to get up there in the turret on a convoy, he knows what to do with the 240."

Kilo Company flew into Kuwait, and stayed there for about two weeks, doing further training to get ready for the move into Iraq. They did PT, bore sighted their weapons, and fired on weapons ranges.

"From Kuwait we headed up to Al Assad. There were three platoons that went up by convoy. Our platoon, 4th Platoon, and H&S Company, took helos, no, we took a C130, up to Al Assad. From Al Assad we took helos, CH 53s, up to where we are right now."

4th Platoon did not stay at Camp Al Qaim very long, they went up to Camp Husaybah for a month with Lima Company. The Army units there told them about the area, and how they did their jobs. Lance Corporal Schultz said that he was lucky enough to go out on one of the Army tanks on a patrol to an OP outside of Husaybah. The platoon helped to fortify the camp in Husaybah. They also began to do foot patrols in the city, and he said that it wasn't too bad, there really wasn't much going on in the way of ambushes or small arms fire. After about a month, they were brought back to Camp Al Qaim.

However, on the first night patrol along with the Army, they got a Frag Order to go on a cordon and knock at a particular house. Lance Corporal Schultz said that he had his NVGs on, but fell into a hole used for repairing cars. He was not hurt, and continued with the patrol. At an IP station, right across from the Baath Party headquarters, they went firm.

"And as we were sitting there firm, we heard a big boom. And there was an RPG, an RPG came down the alley and hit one of the tanks in the turret, and there was small arms that came from the Baath Party house. So the tank opened up with his, I believe, 25 mike mike, and they started suppressing the Baath Party house. Me and another SAW gunner hopped up next to the tank and starting suppressing the Baath

Party house with our SAWs. Then we caught fire, and we ended up just rolling past the Baath Party house there. We didn't want to go in, the Army was still in charge, so they didn't want us to go in because they thought it was booby-trapped."

The patrol continued with the cordon and knock, and took some detainees. These detainees were believed to have been involved in the kidnapping of Iraqis who were working with U.S. forces.

Lance Corporal Schultz said that things remained quiet when the Army left, aside from some IEDs, and he felt safe walking the streets of Husaybah back then. I asked him when this feeling changed. He responded: "The first time I actually felt that I really wasn't that safe was, we came back here, to Camp Al Qaim, and everything was really quiet. I mean, there was nothin', really nothin' goin' on. Until when they were doing mounted patrols through the Sada and Karabilah area, on ASR Diamond. We rolled past the Sada Bluffs early in the evening, and it was still light out, there was a bunch of people, military-age male, nonetheless, standin' on the sides of the roads, by the marketplace. They were kinda huddled in their own little cells, their own little groups. And I looked at 'em and I said to the Marine next to me, my team leader, 'Hey, these guys don't look very friendly around here, do they?' He goes, 'No, they don't.' He goes, 'This'd be a perfect spot for an ambush, too.' 'Cause it's right there by the Sada Bluffs overlookin' the road."

So Schultz's patrol continued past them. On their return, they went past the same area again. It was now dark. They were only about 15 minutes from Camp Al Qaim.

"There was a large explosion. There was an IED, of course. And as soon as that IED went off, an RPG came down the alley between the Sada Bluffs and the eastern edge of the city of Sada. The RPG was within meters of the Humvee that me and our team was in. So, once that RPG went off, a bunch of small arms and RPK came down from off the Sada Bluffs, and started suppressing us. At the same time, we're suppressing them, and we started to dismount. And as we dismount, our lieutenant, Lieutenant Robinson, platoon commander, said he saw somebody runnin' down the hill, so he's screaming for somebody to get a PEC 2, a floodlight on him. The guy ended up gettin' away."

Even with NVGs, it was tough to see into the distance.

Lance Corporal Schultz said that it seemed that the whole eastern edge of the town of Sada was firing from the rooftops. "There was fire comin' from all angles, I mean, it wasn't from one spot."

Schultz was with his squad leader, team leader and several team members. "We came into this one corner and somebody poked their AK 47 around a corner and started shootin' at us, probably about 20 meters away. So we suppressed him, and he ended up getting' away too. I mean, there were guys runnin' all over the neighborhood. But you couldn't see 'em, 'cause they'd shoot, and then they'd run. And they'd shoot, and they'd run. We couldn't see 'em 'cause they'd never show themselves, and we couldn't find them." They then did several cordon and knocks without finding anything.

"Then we decided to push up onto the hill where we got ambushed from, and clear that. So we pushed up that hill, obviously, they [the enemy] were gone, hit and run tactics. We got to the top for an OP, to check out the area. We looked down on the town where we saw the guys runnin' around, we didn't see anything. I'm lookin' through my 17s and I see this guy ridin' in on a donkey, 10 o'clock at night, after a firefight, coming into the area where we got hit. And, he's got a bunch of sheep behind him, and nobody in his right mind's gonna come out riding a donkey after curfew, after a fire fight. So we decide to go down and get him. So we go down there, and we go to this house where he ended up takin' his sheep to, and this guy looks like he's tryin' to climb over the fence, over the big cinderblock wall. So we stop him, tell him to come down, he doesn't come down. We tell him to come down, he doesn't come down. So we sent a Marine over to get him. We ended up getting him, we detained him, and on his donkey, he had had those little pouches that hang out to the side, and we found suspected IED making material."

As the Marines were sitting in the yard setting up 360 degree security, they saw two Iraqis about 20 meters away, running down a hill. There was still small arms fire and RPG fire throughout the city. The ROEs at the time required that the Marines see weapons or hostile intent before they could fire. They could not tell if the Iraqis had weapons. One of them fell, and left something behind. After they were gone, the Marines went out and found that the object was an AK 47 with a sawed-off butt stock! But they were not about to chase after these individuals in the dark into the city. Shortly after this, they did a short sweep further into the city. They found neither weapons nor insurgents.

"We went back to the Humvees that we came from, ASR Diamond that we came from, and, lo and behold, they got IEDs up the road where we dismounted. What happened was, the first IED when it blew, it uprooted two other IEDs that were meant to daisy-chain at the same time, but for some reason they didn't go off. Which we're lucky, 'cause if they did, they woulda killed us all, 'cause they were right where we dismounted."

EOD came and blew the IEDs, and the squad went back to Camp Al Qaim. Lance Corporal Schultz said that they killed one insurgent, and one Marine was killed that night on another ASR near Sada. About five or six IEDs were set off that night. He said it was a coordinated attack.

From then on, Schultz said that the Marines knew that the insurgents were stepping it up, and had different tactics and attack techniques. He knew of an attack that killed the 2nd Squad leader on April 14.

For the big fight on April 17, his squad, 1st Squad, was on React. "My squad was the one that went up there on first React." They went out and took ASR Bronze to go set up just outside the arches at the entrance to Husaybah. "We kinda set up a VCP."

Not many cars were going in or out. They then pushed down to set up another VCP at ASR Diamond. "When we got there, a white conversion van started comin' up our alley, and we told him to stop, and they started firing AKs from their van. So we suppressed that van, the van ended up goin'. Some other Marines took care of it later on down the road."

The squad then set up an OP and didn't let anyone out of the city. Other platoons from Kilo pushed into the city, and his squad joined them and consolidated on East End Road to get ready to push into the city.

"What my squad did was, our squad lined up on this one road, on East End, heading west, and we all pushed. I was rear security, so I was takin' up the rear in case anybody popped out. The guys up in front were takin' some sniper fire, and some guys runnin' across. At the time the Rules of Engagement were, any military age male, between the ages of 16 and 61, they were outside, they were verbally warned, before, not to go outside, they'd be shot."

Insurgents were supposed to be wearing black robes and headbands at the time.

"We saw some people running, not close, but in the distance, we'd take a shot. I shot at a couple people, but there was one time we took a security halt. And I saw this guy peering from the top of a roof, through the little holes, so I pointed my weapon at him and he ducked his head. I kept my weapon in case he poked his head up again. He poked his head out again, I shot at him, he never poked it back out. And then some other head came out over the top of the roof, so I shot him too. He never poked his head back out again."

There were some others he shot at, about 500 meters away.

"I could tell they were up to no good. I saw one black figure, and he was kinda lookin' down the street left and right, to see if it was clear. It was clear, so he started walkin' across. Then another came across. There were like five guys in black robes and head things, so I'm thinking, insurgents, maybe? So I opened up on them, they started runnin' across. I don't know what happened with them."

The squad got to West End Road, and went firm there. They set up an OP in a building in the northwest corner of Husaybah. Schultz said that a convoy came into the area, and there was some miscommunication and friendly fire for about two minutes. He did not say if there were any casualties as a result, but insurgents in the city also joined in the firing.

On April 18, the Marines put the city into a lockdown, and fighting died down. The enemy fighters stopped fighting. Lance Corporal Schultz's squad returned to Camp Al Qaim. Since then, it has been quiet in Husaybah. Schultz said, "I personally think that we sent them a message. They didn't think that we could show that kind of force. Actually, I was talking with one of the translators, this was back in Camp Husaybah, and he said that the people of Iraq, they say that there is a U.S. force, a U.S. Army, the average Iraqi doesn't know up here. Especially in the smaller area, that the average Iraqi doesn't know that there's Marines, there's Army. They think it's just one American force.

"And what they thought when the Army left, with all their big tanks, that we were crazy for walkin' around without any tanks." Also, many thought that the Marines were less strong because they were walking and waving, being nice when they got here. "I think this really changed their mind, once they found out what we could actually do."

I then asked Schultz when he graduated from high school. He replied that it was June 3, 2003. He left for boot camp two weeks later. I said to him that he probably didn't expect to be a combat veteran less than a year later. He said, "I wasn't sure, sir, but I had a pretty good idea."

★ ★ ★

These three days in the Husaybah/Al Qaim area were packed with interviews that filled my journal and notebook with a huge amount of information. Several of the History Division officers who had deployed in 2003 had warned both Major Piedmont and me about staying on top of our interviews, and just as importantly, to document and organize our work as we went along. When we finally returned to Camp Fallujah it took several days to create all required interview file materials. We loaded our digital interview files into our laptops along with photos of every Marine we met. The final step was creating the oral summaries that outlined the main points of each interview, and any cross-references to other Marines' interviews. Every few weeks I would burn updated interview files onto a CD and mail them to the History Division. I did not want to risk losing this information should anything happen to my laptop. Sometimes the challenges in arranging transportation to different units gave us this time to document our work as we went along, but not during the past three days here!

CHAPTER 5

Colonel Tucker, Commanding Officer, RCT7

Thursday June 3, 2004: Camp Al Assad

I had a great, deep sleep at my room in the 3/7 COC building. I got up, packed, had chow, and then learned that my chopper flight for today was a no-go: we had been planning to visit Korean Village today, but the flight was cancelled. If we could get the flight rescheduled for Friday we would stay and do some more interviews here. But around 1100, we had to surrender our room to two other Marine officers. So Major Piedmont and I decided to get on the afternoon flight to Al Assad.

We talked to the air officer and made arrangements to hop the CH 53 flight this afternoon. We got on a bird at 1500, and it took about 40 minutes to get to Al Assad. At RCT7's COC, I hastily made arrangements to interview Colonel Tucker, the RCT commanding officer.

Colonel Craig A. Tucker, Commanding Officer, Regimental Combat Team 7 (RCT7)

This officer commanded all of the Marine ground forces in western Al Anbar province in the summer of 2004. He was the most senior officer that I have had the opportunity to sit down with so far. We met in a large room outside of his office. It had several large leather-covered chairs and a couch. It has been used for meetings with local Iraqi leaders. Colonel Tucker was able to give us a 25-minute interview before he had to go to a meeting. I hoped to get back out here and interview him at greater length, but I never had the opportunity.

I began by asking him about when he learned about OIF II, and what type of preparations he and his staff had done for it. "We started getting hints, I think, we were coming back over here in late summer, September [2003] time frame."

At that time they were planning for an extensive training program through the winter. But, "Word starting getting a little more official in the late September, October time frame. Took a week out of preparations for [Operation] Steel Knight, and Bridgeport, to focus the RCT on, at that time it was the development of a training package if we got the word about going back over to Iraq."

He and his staff drew on the expertise of two of his battalions, 1/7 and 3/7. He wanted to have his Marines trained to respond in a certain way, based on the environment that he expected them to be facing in Iraq. "We trained them in a certain way to respond, to interact with people in the [Iraqi] communities that haven't been in a combat environment. We had to do a certain amount of de-training to teach them things that I call 'habits of thought, habits of action'." Colonel Tucker said that the target was to reach the population of Iraq, to convince the people of the country that we were here for peace.

"The challenge for us is to develop a training program to tie the habit of action, the habit of thought that was focused on two things: One, identifying the targets they kill; Two, not killing anybody that didn't deserve to be killed."

In the course of a week they put this general training idea together, in the event it would be needed. By October, *Steel Knight* had been cancelled, and it was pretty clear that the regiment would be going to Iraq.

In November 2003, he had in operation a training program that started with the squads and worked up to platoon-level operations. "Took 1st Battalion, Seventh Marines [1/7], turned them into a training unit. That's all they did for about two months was train squads and platoons to go into security operations. After Christmas, battalions went in 'The Box' at 29 Palms, then to March Air Force Base for training there."

Another challenge facing Colonel Tucker was how to dispose his forces when they got to Iraq. He was responsible for a huge area of Iraq, and there were issues with civil jurisdiction, tribal issues, and tribal feuds. He made the decision to concentrate on the green belt areas and the border areas.

When his regimental forces started to flow into Iraq, he began the relief with the Army Third ACR.

"Getting here was a pain in the ass. Moving that amount of forces over here, staging them in Kuwait, and driving everybody up here actually went fairly smoothly."

His primary staff got here on February 26, 2004. The battalion staffs had about 10 days to interact with the outgoing Army ACR squadrons.

He noted that, "The Army's approach to this is different than our approach. I make no judgment on that." He said that their structure, weapons and training were much different from the Marines'. Also, the intent of the Marines was to come into the province a little less heavy than the Army units. "The Army did a great job of getting us ready for this hazardous mission."

Colonel Tucker then outlined the task organization of the forces in RCT7. The First LAR Battalion operating in the area is not part of the regiment, but Colonel Tucker worked with their CO in the early 1990s. Tucker noted, "My youngest brother's a sergeant in First LAR."

First Force Reconnaissance Company was in direct support of the regiment: he called it a force multiplier, and it was mostly working with 3/7 up at Al Qaim. Third Battalion, Fourth Marines (3/4) came with a combat-hardened force, as only about 100 of its Marines left after OIF I. It had been preparing to deploy to Okinawa when it was diverted to go to Iraq as part of RCT7. He described this battalion as "a very experienced, cohesive organization. Been together for a long, long time."

Colonel Tucker said that 3/7 was also a fairly experienced battalion, with some new staff. It had participated in SASO operations in Karbala last year in OIF I. The staff, company commanders and experienced corporals leading squads had good working knowledge of the demands of SASO. This was partly why the battalion was operating in far-away Al Qaim, on the western edge of Iraq.

"2/7 is my old battalion, I commanded 2/7 from 1999 to 2001. [They] had an extraordinary challenge at the time. One, we had four battalions at 29 Palms, we only had three here. The battalion did not have equipment, proper 782 gear. We finally got them rifles. The only reason we were able to get them rifles is we traded out the M16 A2s for the A4s. So we got a shipment of A4s and we were able to give them rifles. That's all they had."

Colonel Tucker said that 2/7 did not get all the equipment it needed until mid November. When 2/7 returned from a deployment to Okinawa, there was the normal departure of experienced personnel after arrival in the States. As a result, 2/7 deployed to Iraq with about 650 privates, a very young battalion. The advantage here was that they were eager to learn and train. It also had a new battalion commander, battalion staff, and company commanders. Colonel Tucker placed this battalion out near the western border with Syria, working out of Korean Village with 1st LAR.

"The opening stages of the operation here are pretty much what we expected. We went and did a lot of things that had not been done in the AO before. A couple reasons, one, the intent up the chain of command is that we would have that presence out there. The other thing we're trying to do is kill terrorists—both the networks that facilitate the leadership, the money and weapons. The whole purpose of that is to provide the capability to develop within these communities in Iraq some sort of security base line. So these families can have jobs, kids can go to school, the moms don't have to worry about the kids getting shot on the way to school. Got potable water, got some place to go to the bathroom, just basic, kinda, you need stuff. But the foundation for that is the security environment."

The thought process was to provide this by the presence of the Marines, working along with the Iraqi security forces, whether it be border police, ICDC, or local police. He described this as the "Small Wars" ethos in security operations. A goal was to gain the trust of the people so that they would assist in ridding their communities of what he described as "these bastards."

Colonel Tucker said, "We're starting to see improvements in the Iraqi security forces, we're starting to see interaction that's positive. The people do tell us where the IEDs are located, they do tell us, are willing to tell us, not directly sometimes, but sometimes very subtly, tell us where the elements are that destabilize their communities."

"It depends on the area how much information we learn. That was the basic thought process when the RCT started operations here, but then the nature of the fight changed. It changed from our perspective. I'm not sure if it changed from the enemy's perspective, but it sure changed from our perspective."

"We went out lookin' for bad guys in places we had not been looking before. Inserted ourselves in some areas where there was a 'live and let live' attitude previously. We kicked over an ant pile, that we kicked over in Fallujah, that we kicked over early in Husaybah, we kicked it over on the 9th [of April]. I think we got a little too much pressure. And that pressure was Marine Corps presence, and the pressure was also the fact they realized that we weren't randomly waiting for rape and killin' of women and children in the streets [by the insurgents]. And we had that kinda face-to-face interaction with the Iraqis. Weren't driving on Bradleys and tanks."

The Marines had started to have a positive impact, and Colonel Tucker felt that that, combined with the Marines' presence in the cities, and the Sadr militia actions, seemed to cause the insurgents to feel driven to act.

Colonel Tucker felt that the approaching turnover of sovereignty on July 1 2004 may have been a factor in the violence that took place in Al Anbar in April. He was not sure about this, however. He wondered if the uprisings were coordinated across the province.

At any rate, he said, "He [the enemy] came in April, got his ass kicked, made some significant mistakes. Underestimated, I think, it's interesting. Underestimated the ferocity of the Marine rifle squad, platoon, company, infantry battalion. I think they equated power to tanks and Bradleys. I think he observed some of the things we were doing, tactics, candy patrols, and walkin' around the street bein' nice to people, as a sign of weakness. I'm convinced, that what happened out in Husaybah, happened, they made a decision to make that attack relatively quickly. I don't think it was planned at that period of time." He felt that the enemy made the decision to attack on April 9 when elements of the RCT were sent east to the vicinity of Fallujah. "We pulled the tanks out, we pulled the AAVs out, we took the LAVs out, all we had left was a Marine rifle battalion. They underestimated that."

★ ★ ★

With that, Colonel Tucker had to break off the interview, as he had another staff meeting to attend. However, his words had helped to create a better picture of the events in Husaybah in April. On my later visits to RCT7 units, I would get to fill in some of the questions I had in interviews with Marines there.

As it began to get darker, RCT7 provided Major Piedmont and me a driver to get to the PAX terminal, and we waited two hours there for the "Jailbird" (call sign) CH46 flight. We made about five stops at different Marine camps before getting to Fallujah. Five minutes out of Al Assad, we took ground fire—or so I thought (I saw four or five flashes on the ground) and a .50 cal on the chopper engaged them. Turns out that this was merely the gunner of our chopper test firing his .50 caliber machine gun! The flashes on the ground were his .50 cal rounds impacting.

At Hurricane Point outside of Ramadi, the chopper's ASE gear sent orange/red flares from the tail of the bird while we were taking off. I later found out that sometimes these flares shoot off at unexpected times. Either way, it was excitement that I didn't need. The bird got us into Camp Fallujah around 0030, and we checked in at the EFCAT (Enduring Freedom Combat Assessment Team, that had provided us support for our oral history mission) tent to let them know we were back. I then went to my room, locked up my pistol, dropped onto the cot and fell right asleep. It had been another busy cluster of days with the Marines of 3/7, packed with interviews, travel, and uncertainty as to where I would be each night—just another week in the life as a field historian during a deployment. Every day brought many challenges, from arranging travel to coordinating schedules with Marines in action, and getting briefed on the latest actions and plans. Infantry battalions and companies could be called to deploy to a different region or mission at a moment's notice. A key element in interview efforts was remaining flexible in getting to meet the Marines, and also the ability to stay mentally sharp by getting rest when possible. The reward was being able to meet with and record the words of so many remarkable young men.

Final Thoughts

My days of meetings and interviews with some of the Marines of 3/7 painted a picture of a well-trained, adaptable force. As conditions on the ground changed after their arrival, they changed their approach. From planned Security and Stability Operations, they quickly transitioned to full combined arms combat operations. Marines in every MOS moved to the sound of the guns to confront enemy forces and support their fellow Marines.

Many of the Marines interviewed had been involved in the invasion of Iraq in 2003. I included their recollections of those events, as well as short recaps of their military backgrounds, to give a fuller picture of the more recent operations. Many other off-the-record conversations with Marines in units at all levels helped me to better focus my questions for those I digitally recorded. My interviews were done on unclassified topics. This was partially because I was constantly moving from camp to camp, and I did not have access to secure equipment or facilities to store or transport classified materials such as interview files or maps. I was careful not to photograph maps in briefing areas, or any command posts or Combat Operations Centers.

The tours of Marine units in Iraq during 2004 lasted seven months. These deployments were shorter than the U.S. Army's 12-month deployments, but Marine leadership felt strongly that this allowed the Marines to remain focused and fresh throughout their tours. It also allowed the Marine Corps to maintain its other worldwide deployment obligations.

Things had quieted down in Husaybah while I was in Iraq, even until my return to the U.S. in August 2004. The following April (2005), there would again be major fighting in this border city. But again, Marine units there would respond effectively to the threats.

I remain inspired and humbled after meeting so many of these dedicated young men who placed themselves at the "tip of the spear" while in Iraq.

Currently, all of the 190 interviews that I conducted during my deployment in Iraq are in storage at the Marine Corps' History Center in Quantico, Virginia. The slow process of transcribing them, along with several thousand other interviews done by members of the Field History detachment in 2003 and 2004, continues. Many thousands of Oral History interviews were done by deployed officers of the Field History detachment during and after operations in 2003 when the Marines first fought in Iraq. In 2004, only two Marine Corps field historians deployed in the spring and summer (Major John Piedmont and me), followed by Captain Joseph Winslow that fall. Captain Winslow was deployed to the Fallujah area during Operation Phantom Fury.

One cause for concern is that as computer software constantly evolves, it may become difficult to access digital recordings created in 2004. The challenge at the History Center is to keep these interview files accessible into future years.

All Marine Corps Field History digital interview files have a written Interview Documentation Sheet (see Appendix) and a digital recording of the interview, along with a photograph of the subject Marine or sailor. Copies of award citations, when available at the time of the interview, are also included. Each summary also includes cross-references to other interview subjects, making it easier to find different perspectives by participants in many significant actions. These oral history files are available to researchers and writers. My hope is to produce more short volumes like this one to tell more of the stories of the Marines and sailors I met, and to make the public aware of this valuable resource: The Marine Corps Oral History Program.

One of the frustrating things while working on the final stages of producing this book was that so little supporting material—relevant combat images, maps, and other published stories about Husaybah 2004—is available. The archives section at the Marine Corps History Division was unable to find any digital images of combat there during the 2004 time period. Neither did the Marine Corps History Division have any detailed maps of the 2004 fights in Husaybah. One map that I used when drafting my manuscript were taken from a website (*Danger Close* http://lima37.com/blog/2009/02/01/chapter-10-battle-of-husaybah/.) that seemed to have been maintained by someone outside of official Marine Corps channels, and is no longer on the Internet. I used Situation Maps from this site to later have a graphics artist create the Husaybah situation map for this book.

Also, of the 190 or so interviews that I conducted, none have been used by any author that I know of in their writings about the Iraq war. During my deployment I met with Marines who referred to their personal journals and notes during interview sessions, and often used a Situation Map in an office to illustrate the actions they described. The memories were fresh in their minds. These in-the-field oral history interviews contain vivid details unsullied by time, much more vivid than phone conversations held a long time after the events.

Some of the Marines who I interviewed in the days and weeks after the events were indeed interviewed by book authors, but usually years later, and often via phone. Memories do fade in time, making some of these recollections of a different value than those recorded in the immediate aftermath of the events.

The Marines of 3/7 operated without any combat camera assets during April 2004. The First Marine Expeditionary Force (IMEF) did supply individual units with then-new digital cameras. Despite the widespread availability of these cameras, their photographs were mostly used in after-action reports of damage caused during combat operations, or used by division and MEF planners for continued planning. The 3/7 Marines engaged in combat were busy being engaged in combat, and did not have the luxury of taking photographs or videos during their fights. On the other hand, actions in Fallujah during this time were extensively covered by military combat camera as well as civilian media camera assets there.

This was part of my motivation to write these "ground level" stories that sometimes receive a paragraph or sentence mention in many of the publications about events at this time in Iraq. There are many excellent books (see Sources and Further Reading) covering so much of the combat in that country, but almost no mention of the 2004 fighting in Husaybah. The stories in this book are on-the-ground perspectives of the intense combat in Husaybah that has been largely overlooked in major publications about the conflict in Iraq during 2004. There remains an untapped trove of thousands of field history interviews with Marines and sailors that contains many amazing stories, just waiting to be told.

Interview Documentation Sheet

Captain Dominique Baissou Neal   **Date: 2 June 2004**

Interview Documentation Sheet

Interviewer: Lieutenant Colonel David Kelly, USMC

Date of interview: 2 June 2004

Summary written by: Lieutenant Colonel David Kelly, USMC

Subject: Captain Dominique Baissou Neal
                            Company Commander
                            Lima Company, 3/7

Location of Interview: Camp Husaybah, Iraq

Recording format: DSS file

Length of interview: 1:12:03

Corresponding materials: Interview with Lt. Bradley R. Watson, 3rd Platoon Commander, Lima Company (2 June 2004)

Have you included materials other than the recording?   Yes

Briefly describe quantity and types of other materials: Digital photo of interview subject, VIRIN 040602-M-9464-K-006. Photo caption: Captain Dominique B. Neal assumed command of Lima Company 3-7, when company commander Captain Rich Gannon was killed in combat operations in fighting in Husaybah, Iraq, in mid April 2004. (Official Marine Corps Photo by LtCol David Kelly)

Classification: Unclassified

Main subjects and keywords of the interview: Captain Dominique Neal, Company Commander, Lima Company 3/7, Operation Iraqi Freedom II-1, Husaybah, IED (Improvised Explosive Device).

Briefly Summarize Interview:
Personal info: USNA graduate, with 3/7 entire time in Marine Corps after schools. (2:00)
OIF II-1
Training for return to Iraq included SASO, and MOUT training at March AFB.
Lima Company designated at main effort for 3/7, Company Commander Captain Rich Gannon was senior company commander in battalion, meticulous planner, gave lots of responsibility to (then) Lieutenant Neal , company Executive Officer.
Capt. Gannon used Lt. Neal as an XO and an Ops O.
Attachments to company due to relatively remote location (20:00) given.
In mid-April, mood in area grew tense, intell sources warned of uptick in enemy actions, IEDs became a bigger threat.

Captain Dominique Baissou Neal   **Date: 2 June 2004**

Lima Co. modified patrol schedule, more aggressive.
14 April – Contacts with enemy.
17 April – Camp Husaybah attacked with 25 mortar rounds. Battalion S 3 happened to be at camp that day. (then) Lieutenant Neal begins to get needed ammo to units, acts without word from CO. Hopes that Capt. Gannon was alive somewhere, even though not heard from in hours. Touching description of his feelings when he learns of death of Capt Gannon, the CO. (50:30) Battalion commences a sweep through Husaybah late that day (from East to West), mortars, and Close Air Support (Cobra & Huey helos) used.
April 18 – Lima Company assigned to Eastern part of Husaybah for Battalion sweep from North to South. Searched all houses in sector – company felt good on the sweep.
Captain Neal was frocked to current rank by Battalion commander, LtCol Matt Lopez.
Operations currently less intense, locals seem more friendly (or less hostile), less IEDs in area.
ICDC (Iraqi Civil Defense Corps) & police working alongside Marines.

Interviewer Comments:
Incredible interview!
Starts slowly with overview of task organization of Lima Company 3/7 and planned role in western Iraq at Camp Husaybah on the Syrian border.
 Beginning at 35:30 of recording, detailed description of actions in the company Combat Operations Center in Husaybah, and last radio contact with company commander Captain Gannon (45:00), re-supplying platoons that needed ammo, to learning that Capt Gannon was dead (50:30): "Lima 6 is routine" (evacuation). Routine evacuation can mean either not seriously wounded, or deceased.

Glossary

203	M203 single-shot 40mm grenade launcher, under barrel attachment to a rifle
240 Golf	M240 belt-fed, gas-operated machine gun firing a 7.62mm belt-fed round. Rate of fire 650 to 950 rounds per minute
.50 caliber machine gun	Browning M2 machine gun
7th Comm	7th Communication Battalion. Provides communication network for various Marine forces
7-ton MTVR	Medium Tactical Replacement Vehicle. Tactical truck with a 7-ton capacity.
782 gear	Field equipment issued to individual Marines. Refers to the form DD 782, signed when gear is issued
AAV	Amphibious Assault Vehicle, AAV P7. Fully tracked amphibious landing vehicle. Armament includes M 19 40mm automatic grenade launcher, and M2 .50 caliber machine gun. See "Amtrak"
ACOG	Advanced Combat Optical Gun sight for the M16 and M4 rifle

ACR	Armored Cavalry Regiment of the U.S. Army
A-Driver	Assistant Driver on any road vehicle
AK 47	*Avtomat Kalashnikova.* Soviet-designed assault rifle firing a 7.62mm round. Commonly called Kalashnikov
Amtrak	Nickname for Marine Amphibious Assault Vehicle (AAV)
AO	Area of Operations
ASR	Alternate Supply Road
AT4	84mm unguided, portable recoilless smoothbore rocket. Common anti-tank weapon
BAS	Battalion Aid Station. A medical section within a battalion's support company
Bird	Nickname for any helicopter
Blackhawk	UH-60 Medium-lift Helicopter of the U.S. Army
Blade 6	Radio call sign for 3/7's commander, Lieutenant Colonel Lopez
Bradley Fighting Vehicle (BFV)	Family of U.S. Army armored fighting vehicles with a crew of three and room for six soldiers
BZO	Battle Sight Zero. Adjusting the sight settings for the rifle
C4	Variety of plastic explosive
CAAT	Combined Anti-Armor Team. Task-organized from elements of a Weapons Company

CAS	Close air support. Air support by fixed wing or rotary wing aircraft of ground actions in close proximity to friendly forces
CASEVAC	Casualty evacuation
CASH or CSH	Military Combat Support Hospital
CAX	Combined Arms Exercise. Conducted at Marine Corps Base 29 Palms, California
CCP	Casualty Collection Point
Claymore mine	A directional anti-personnel mine, fired by wired remote control
Click	1,000 meters on a standard military map
COC	Combat Operations Center
CP	Command Post
Cobra	Bell AH-1W Super Cobra Attack Helicopter. Weapons systems can include 20mm M197 3-barrel Gatling gun, 2.75mm Hydra 70 rockets, 5" Zuni rockets, TOW missiles, AGM 114 Hellfire missiles, AIM-9 Sidewinder anti-aircraft missiles
Deck	Naval term that Marines also use to describe any land surface
Dragunov	SVD Soviet sniper rifle. Effective range of up to 800 meters. Fires a 7.62 round
EAS	End of active service
EFCAT	Enduring Freedom Combat Assessment Team. In 2004 based at Quantico, Virginia. Sent teams to Iraq and Afghanistan to collect "Lessons Learned" relating to Marine

	Corps participation in Operation Enduring Freedom and Operation Iraqi Freedom
EOD	Explosive Ordnance Disposal
ER	Emergency Room
EWS	Expeditionary Warfare School. A 41-week residential course for company grade officers at Quantico, Virginia. Formerly AWS— Amphibious Warfare School
FAC	Forward Air Controller: a Marine aviator assigned to ground units to insure that close air support hits intended targets and does not harm friendly troops
FAST Team	Fleet Anti-terrorism Support Team
Fire team	Marine infantry organization of four Marines. Part of a 12-man squad
Firm Base	Small, austere outpost. "Going firm" is creating a hasty defense when stopped for a short time
Fixed wing	Jet aircraft
Flak jacket/flak	Sleeveless jacket reinforced with Kevlar, protects against bullets and shrapnel
Fleet	Fleet Marine Force. Operational forces of the U.S. Marines
FOB	Forward Operating Base
Frag	Fragmentation grenade
Frag order	A hasty order for an action (fragmentary order)
Frag wound	Fragment wound caused by shrapnel

Frock	Temporary promotion to higher rank before normal promotion date to fill a billet
FRSS	U.S. Navy's Forward Resuscitative Surgery System
FSSG	Force Service Support Group. Provides combat service support for a Marine Expeditionary Force (MEF)
Glock	9mm semiautomatic pistol
Gunny	Nickname for a Marine Gunnery Sergeant (E7)
HESCO Barriers	A barrier made of collapsible wire mesh filled with earth, gravel or rock, to create a defensive barrier
H&S Company	Headquarters and Service Company
HET	Human Exploitation Team that includes translators. Provided by U.S. Army
HIND rocket	Soviet-designed air-to-ground missile, S-5. Has a variety of warheads including HE (high explosive), smoke, and incendiary rounds
HK triangle	Husaybah-Karabilah road triangle between the two towns
HKS 433	Heckler-Koch assault weapon firing a 5.56mm round
HM	U.S. Navy Hospital Corpsman. HM3 is a Petty Officer Third Class (E 4)
Humvee	The High Mobility Multipurpose Wheeled Vehicle (HMMWV, nicknamed Humvee) is a family of light, four-wheel drive, military trucks and utility vehicles produced by AM General

Humint	Human Intelligence gained from contact with individuals
Hummer	Nickname for Humvee truck
ICDC	Iraqi Civil Defense Corps; became the Iraqi National Guard after the turnover of sovereignty at the end of June 2004
IED	Improvised explosive device
Intel	Intelligence
IO	Information Operations, and public relations
IOC	Infantry Officer Course, at Quantico, Virginia. Challenging course to screen Marine second lieutenants seeking the infantry MOS 0302
IP	Iraqi Police
Karabilah	Small town in Al Qaim area near Husaybah.
Karbala	A large city about 62 miles southwest of Baghdad.
KIA	Killed in Action
LAR	Light Amphibious Reconnaissance. Armored mobilized land reconnaissance unit. Used to gather intelligence and for screening. Marines use the LAV 25 (Light Amphibious Vehicle) as its main vehicle
Left-seat, Right-seat	Technique in which U.S. Army personnel give familiarization rides in vehicles to incoming Marines. During early rides the soldiers lead, then Marines ride in lead positions.

LZ	Landing Zone, area set aside for helicopter landings
M 19	40mm automatic grenade launcher
MCRD	Marine Corps Recruit Depot. The Corps has two: One in San Diego, CA, and one in Parris Island, SC
MECEP	Marine Enlisted College Entrance Prep School. Program held in summers to prepare selected Marine NCOs for college completion and commissioning as officers
MEF	Marine Expeditionary Force. Largest Marine air-ground task force. Includes a Command Element, a Ground Combat element (Marine division), a Marine Air Wing, and a Marine Logistics Group. IMEF is based out of Camp Pendleton, California
MEU	Marine Expeditionary Unit. Smallest Marine air-ground task force. Usually based around a reinforced infantry battalion and attached elements
MHG	Marine Headquarters Group of a Marine Expeditionary Force (MEF)
Midrats	Midnight rations, usually served for nighttime watch-standers on a Navy ship
MOI	Marine officer instructor. An officer on the NROTC (Naval Reserve Officer Training Corps) staff at a college or university. Supervises midshipmen who opt for a Marine officer commission
MOUT	Military Operations in Urban Terrain

MOPP suit	Mission-Oriented Protective Posture equipment. In the 2003 invasion, this included gas mask, protective suit, gloves and boot covers
MOS	Military Occupational Specialty
Motor T	Motor transport
MP	Military Police
MPF	Maritime pre-positioning program. Strategic power-projection capability to provide most of the combat equipment needed for two Marine Expeditionary Brigades (MEBs)
MREs	Meals Ready to Eat. Rations for operations in the field
Mujahideen	Muslim guerrilla forces
NCO	Non-commissioned senior enlisted member
NVGs	Night vision goggles
OCS	Officer Candidate School. A 10-week screening and selection program for college graduates to obtain commissions as Marine second lieutenants. Most Marine officers are obtained through this program. Also OCC (Officer Candidates' Course)
ODA	Operational Detachment Alpha, a U.S. Army Special Forces team
OP	Observation Post
Op Order	Operations Order. A standard Five-Paragraph Order for the conduct of operations (See SMEAC)

PFC	Private First Class. Enlisted rank (E2)
PLC	Platoon Leaders' Course. A screening and selection program for college students. Held each summer at Quantico, Virginia. Successful candidates receive officer commissions after college graduation
PRR Radio	Personal Role Radio. Range of up to 500 meters
PSYOPS	U.S. Army Psychological Operations. Specialists who assess the information needs of a civilian population and craft messages to influence them
PT	Physical training
PX	Post Exchange. A base retail store. In remote FOBs, often offering toiletries and personal items for sale
QRF	Quick Reaction Force. Any task-organized unit ready to respond to another unit in contact with enemy forces
RCT	Regimental Combat Team. Marine infantry regiment with attached and supporting elements that allow it to be self-supporting in the field
RTC	U.S. Navy Recruit Training Command
RO	Radio Operator
ROEs	Rules of Engagement in a conflict
RPG	Shoulder-fired rocket-propelled grenade
RPK	Soviet-designed light machine gun, fires a 7.62mm round

SAPI plates	Small Arms Protective Insert. Placed into ballistic vests (flak jackets) to intercept projectiles and some explosive fragments
SASO	Security and Stability Operations
SAW	Squad Automatic Weapon. M249 Light machine gun. Belt-fed, firing a 5.56mm round, has a quick-change barrel
SCUD	Soviet-designed tactical missile
Sitrep	Situation report of an ongoing action
Skipper	Nickname for commanding officer of a Marine infantry company
Small Wars Manual	U.S. Marine Corps manual on tactics and strategies for engaging in certain types of military operations
SMAW	Mark 153 Shoulder-launched Multipurpose Assault Weapon. A shoulder-launched rocket used primarily to destroy bunkers and fortifications
SOI	School of Infantry. Second stage of military training for Marines who have completed Basic Training
SMEAC	Acronym for the organization of a Marine Corps' Five-Paragraph Order: Situation, Mission, Execution, Administration & Logistics, Control
SPC	Staff Platoon Commander. An officer who supervises training a platoon of new Marine lieutenants at The Basic School in Quantico
SOP	Standard Operating Procedure

STA	Surveillance and Target Acquisition. Provide surveillance and Scout-Sniper teams
Staff NCO	Staff Non-Commissioned Officer. An enlisted Marine with rank of E6
STP	Shock Trauma Platoon
Staff Organizations	S1 Personnel/manpower S2 Intelligence or security S3 Operations S4 Logistics or supply S5 Plans S6 Communications
TBS	The Basic School at Quantico, Virginia. A 26-week course. Provides training for all newly commissioned Marine second lieutenants prior to further MOS training
T/O	Table of Organization. Personnel designated to a unit
Trak	Nickname for a Marine AAV
T-Rats	Tray Rations. Pre-packaged rations not requiring refrigeration. Food is in large sealed aluminum trays heated in hot water. May be prepared where a field kitchen does not exist. Each tray can contain food for 36 Marines
TSB	Transportation Support Battalion. Provide transportation and throughput support for a Marine Expeditionary Force (MEF)
TTPs	Tactics, Techniques and Procedures

UGR (M)	UGR-M (formerly UGR-B) is the primary group ration for the Marine Corps. It meets the Marines' expeditionary requirements for high-quality group rations that are shelf stable (no refrigeration needed), quick and easy to prepare
UXO	Unexploded Ordnance
VCP	Vehicle Checkpoint
VIP	Very Important Person. Often a high-ranking officer
WIA	Wounded in Action
Wing	Elements of Marine Aviation, fixed wing or helicopter
XO	Executive Officer in a military unit company size and above

Sources and Further Reading

Field History Journal of Lieutenant Colonel David E. Kelly, March–July 2004 (On file with US Marine Corps History and Museums Division)
Interview Notes of Lieutenant Colonel David E. Kelly (Author's collection)

Field History Interviews by the Author

Colonel Craig A. Tucker, USMC, Camp Al Assad, Iraq, 06/03/2004
Lieutenant Colonel Matthew A. Lopez, USMC, Camp Al Assad, Iraq, 05/31/2004
Commander Edward W. Hessell, USN, MD, Camp Al Qaim, Iraq, 06/01/2004
Captain Dominique B. Neal, USMC, FOB Camp Husaybah, Iraq, 06/02/2004
Captain Bradford W. Tippett, USMC, Camp Al Qaim, Iraq, 06/01/2004
Lieutenant Bradley R. Watson, USMC, FOB Camp Husaybah, Iraq, 06/02/2004
First Sergeant Michael J. Templeton, USMC, Camp Al Qaim, Iraq, 06/03/2004
Gunnery Sergeant Brian W. Eyestone, USMC, Camp Al Qaim, Iraq, 06/01/2004
Staff Sergeant Alexander A. Carlson, USMC, Camp Al Qaim, Iraq, 06/01/2004
Staff Sergeant Ronnie Lee King, USMC Camp Al Qaim, Iraq, 06/01/2004
Corporal Kristopher E. Benson, USMC, Camp Al Qaim, Iraq, 06/01/2004
Corporal Christopher Logan Cahill, USMC, Camp Al Qaim, Iraq, 06/01/2004
Corporal Ryan D. Griffey, USMC, Camp Al Qaim, Iraq, 06/01/2004
Corporal Jason A. Lemcke, USMC, FOB Camp Husaybah, Iraq, 06/02/2004
Corporal Michael T. Phillips, USMC, Camp Al Qaim, Iraq, 06/01/2004
HM3 Justin T. Purviance, USN, FOB Camp Husaybah, Iraq, 06/02/2004
Lance Corporal Jerad D. Allen, USMC, Camp Al Qaim, Iraq, 06/01/2004
Lance Corporal Daniel P. Baute, USMC, Camp Al Qaim, Iraq, 06/01/2004
Lance Corporal Daniel R. Johnston, USMC, FOB Camp Husaybah, Iraq, 06/02/2004
Lance Corporal Jason A. Sanders, USMC, Camp Al Qaim, Iraq, 06/01/2004
Lance Corporal Brian M. Schultz, USMC, Camp Al Qaim, Iraq, 06/03/2004
Lance Corporal Jonathon D. Stamper, USMC, Camp Al Qaim, Iraq, 06/03/2004

Further Reading on Conflict in Iraq

Camp, Dick, *Operation Phantom Fury: The Assault and Capture of Fallujah, Iraq*, Minneapolis, MN, Zenith Press, 2009

Estes, Kenneth W., Lieutenant Colonel, USMC (Ret.), *U.S. Marine Corps Operations in Iraq, 2003–2006*, Washington, DC, History Division Marine Corps University, 2009

Estes, Kenneth W., Lieutenant Colonel USMC (Ret.), *US Marines in Iraq 2004–2005 Into the Fray*, Washington, DC,History Division Marine Corps University, 2011

Lowry, Richard S., *New Dawn: The Battles for Fallujah*, New York, Savas Beattie, 2010

O'Donnell, Patrick K., *We Were One*, Boston, Da Capo Press, 2006

Reynolds, Nicholas E., Colonel, USMC (Ret.), *Basrah, Baghdad, and Beyond – The US Marine Corps in the Second Iraq War*, Annapolis, Maryland, Naval Institute Press, 2009

Schlosser, Dr. Nicholas J., *US Marines in Iraq 2004–2008: Anthology and Annotated Bibliography*, Washington, DC, History Division Marine Corps University, 2010

Schlosser, Dr. Nicholas J., *US Marines in Battle: Al Qaim September 2005–March 2006*, Washington, DC, History Division Marine Corps University, 2013

West, Bing, *No True Glory: A Frontline Account of the Battle for Fallujah*, New York, Bantam Books, 2005

The Author

Lieutenant Colonel David E. Kelly retired from the Marine Corps Reserve in 1999 after a 29-year career, both active and reserve. His last assignment prior to retirement was as operations officer for the Marine Corps Field History Detachment that operated out of the Washington, DC, Navy Yard. In that billet he planned training for Marine Corps field historians, and also contributed to the Marine Corps 1998 commemorative anthology, *Marines in the Spanish American War.*

In late 2003, he agreed to return to active duty in order to deploy to Iraq as one of only two Marine field historians there. During the planning stages that year, the Marine Corps trained for Security and Stability Operations, but events would overtake this planning as a full-scale insurgency began in the spring of 2004. During a five-month deployment, Lieutenant Colonel Kelly and Major John Piedmont traveled to interview Marines in all areas of Iraq.

Upon completion of the deployment, all oral interviews and photographs were downloaded onto CDs and filed at the Marine Corps Oral History division. The collection is now located at Quantico, Virginia.

He "re-retired" on the completion of his deployment, and returned to civilian life in the fall of 2004. He then began to review his copies of these interviews and personal journal to create this book.

Lieutenant Colonel David E. Kelly retired in June 2017 as high school history teacher at Cardinal O'Hara High School in Springfield, Pennsylvania.

Index